At Issue

| Polygamy

Other Books in the At Issue Series:

At Issue

Polygamy

Ronnie D. Lankford, Jr., Book Editor

GREENHAVEN PRESS
A part of Gale, Cengage Learning

GALE
CENGAGE Learning·

Detroit • New York • San Francisco • New Haven, Conn • Waterville, Maine • London

Christine Nasso, *Publisher*
Elizabeth Des Chenes, *Managing Editor*

© 2009 Greenhaven Press, a part of Gale, Cengage Learning.

Gale and Greenhaven Press are registered trademarks used herein under license.

For more information, contact:
Greenhaven Press
27500 Drake Rd.
Farmington Hills, MI 48331-3535
Or you can visit our Internet site at gale.cengage.com

Articles in Greenhaven Press anthologies are often edited for length to meet page requirements. In addition, original titles of these works are changed to clearly present the main thesis and to explicitly indicate the author's opinion. Every effort is made to ensure that Greenhaven Press accurately reflects the original intent of the authors. Every effort has been made to trace the owners of copyrighted material.

Cover photograph © Images.com/Corbis.

LIBRARY OF CONGRESS CATALOGING-IN-PUBLICATION DATA

Polygamy / Ronnie D. Lankford, book editor.
    p. cm. -- (At issue)
    Includes bibliographical references and index.
    ISBN-13: 978-0-7377-4106-3 (hardcover)
    ISBN-13: 978-0-7377-4107-0 (pbk.)
    1. Polygamy. I. Lankford, Ronald D., 1962-
    HQ981.P646 2009
    306.84'23--dc22

                                                    2008014668

Printed in the United States of America
1 2 3 4 5 6 7 13 12 11 10 09

Contents

Introduction

Until recently, polygamy in the United States and Canada has been associated with 19th century history. Mormons practiced polygamy legally in North America until it was banned in Canada in 1867 and in the United States in 1879. Within the last several years, however, polygamy has become a widely covered news item. The trial of Warren Jeffs, the spiritual leader of the Fundamentalist Church of Jesus Christ of Latter Day Saints (FLDS), and HBO's series *Big Love*, have reminded many that polygamy is still practiced in the United States and Canada today. Multiple news stories have also covered the prospering polygamist community of Bountiful, British Columbia, and, increasingly, commentators have wondered whether the legalization of same-sex marriage will lead to the legalization of polygamy.

This attention, however, often leaves readers with more questions than answers. How many people are practicing polygamy or living within polygamous communities in North America? Do the communities and individuals who practice polygamy come from Mormon splinter groups or from a variety of religious backgrounds? If the practice of polygamy is illegal in both the United States and Canada, why has it continued to exist and, some critics contend, grow? While the answers to these questions are complex, they nonetheless provide a springboard to understanding the practice of plural marriage in North America today.

Because polygamy is illegal in both Canada and the United States, obtaining exact numbers of persons practicing polygamy is difficult. Many who practice plural marriage do so in secrecy. According to National Public Radio, estimates have ranged from 20,000 to 50,000 in North America. The *Salt Lake Tribune* has estimated that there are 37,000 fundamentalist Mormons in the western United States alone, half of whom live in polygamous families. Anne Wilde of Principle Voices of Polygamy has suggested that polygamous populations of Mormon splinter groups have continued to grow during the last ten years.

Polygamy is most visible in isolated communities like Bountiful, British Columbia, and Colorado City, Arizona. Founded in 1947 and primarily consisting of members of the FLDS, the Bountiful community has grown to approximately 1,000 members. Colorado City, Arizona, a community of 4,600 persons, is made up of three different Mormon splinter groups. Many individuals, however, practice polygamy more quietly. "There are several ultra-orthodox offshoots of the Mormon Church . . . especially in rural parts of Utah, which quietly practice polygamy today basically under a 'Don't Ask, Don't Tell' policy," noted writer Del Leu. "Most polygamists just want to be left alone and don't want notoriety."

In the past, many people have assumed that polygamy was related to the Church of Jesus Christ of Latter-day Saints (LDS). This assumption is complicated, however, by the fact that the LDS discontinued the doctrine of plural marriage in 1890. The church, however, has had many splinter groups, some who found their own churches by choice and others who have been ejected from the LDS. While Mormon splinter groups may be visible in Bountiful and Colorado City (especially the FLDS), people from a multitude of religious and ethnic backgrounds also practice polygamy today.

In the spring of 2007 the *New York Times* reported on a deadly house fire that revealed the presence of a polygamous family that had emigrated from Mali. "Immigration to New York and other American cities has soared from places where polygamy is lawful and widespread, especially from West African countries like Mali, where demographic surveys show that 43 percent of women are in polygamous marriages," wrote Nina Bernstein in the *New York Times*.

In 2007 the *San Francisco Chronicle* reported on a number of African American Muslims who had chosen to live polygamous lifestyles. Some commentaries have justified the choice within the African American community because of what is referred to as the "male shortage," created by the incarceration of many young African American males. As with the *New York Times*, the *San Francisco Chronicle* also noted an increase in immigrants practicing polygamy. "Plural marriages exist in majority Muslim populations of Africa and the Persian Gulf states," wrote Pauline Bartolone in the *San Francisco Chronicle*, "and immigrants continue the practice in the United States."

A basic question surrounding the practice of polygamy puzzles many onlookers: if polygamy is illegal in the United States and Canada, then why have so many people been able to practice it with impunity? Despite the attention that has been brought to the Bountiful community, the Canadian government has been reluctant to file a suit. And while the prosecution of Warren Jeffs has been a high-profile case in the United States, it has revolved around Jeffs's role in arranging marriages for underage girls, not polygamy. Most polygamists in North America are simply left alone by legal authorities.

Critics offer various reasons why authorities ignore these infractions. On one level, past attempts to prosecute polygamous communities, such as a raid on Colorado City in 1953, have proven problematic. The media coverage of the raid was largely sympathetic to the polygamists, and the trial extended for two years and, many believed, ruined Governor John Howard Pyle's political career. On another level, the sheer numbers of practitioners, many who are not easily identified, make prosecution impractical. Finally, if federal authorities in the United States and Canada choose to prosecute persons practicing polygamy, the possibility exists that antiplural marriage laws might be struck down as an infringement on the freedom of religion.

The practice of polygamy has deep religious and cultural roots. While dissident Mormon sects may have once been considered the sole practitioners in North America, today Muslims, Christians, and many immigrants practice plural marriage. Overall, the number of persons living in polygamous communities may be small, but these communities have long histories and a dedication to maintaining their lifestyles. Polygamy has survived and even prospered despite restrictions and occasional prosecution from civil and religious authorities.

While essays within this book focus on questions such as whether polygamy will be legalized in the near future, many individuals and groups are intent on practicing plural marriage regardless of its legality. Furthermore, as recent history has proven, there seems little likelihood that polygamists will be prosecuted. In a sense, then, the current debate over polygamy has less to do with whether multiple religious and cultural groups will continue to practice polygamy than whether American and Canadian cultures are willing to broaden the traditional understanding of marriage and family.

1

Polygamists Should Be Tolerated

Richard Mouw

Richard Mouw has served as president of Fuller Theological Seminary since 1993.

There are many beliefs that one might not agree with, but in a free society, we should allow others to practice these beliefs nonetheless. Many have argued that spousal abuse is common in polygamous relationships, but spousal abuse is also common in monogamous relationships. It is also hypocritical to make polygamy illegal when many Americans legally practice serial monogamy (they marry, divorce, then remarry). Even if one does not personally approve of polygamy, one might still admire a religious group like the Mormons who place a high value on family and community.

For almost four decades in the nineteenth century, the Mormon community officially sanctioned polygamy (the more common term among Mormons is "plural marriage"). The Church of Jesus Christ of Latter-day Saints (LDS) finally banned the practice in the 1890s, a decision that paved the way for Utah to be granted statehood. But Mormon polygamy never really disappeared. Splinter groups of Mormon "fundamentalists" have continued to practice plural marriage. And now the subject is in the news because one of these dissidents—an outspoken husband of at least five wives—is being tried as a criminal for his polygamous lifestyle.

Richard Mouw, "A Modest Defense of Polygamy," *BeliefNet.com*, 2006. Reproduced by permission.

There aren't too many folks willing to defend the rights of the Mormon dissidents. Mainstream LDS members would rather not have the spotlight aimed at their own past sanction of plural marriage. Many feminists, inspired by reports about abuse of women in plural marriages, have portrayed polygamous wives as victims of "enslavement." Nor have the leaders of Protestant, Catholic, and Jewish groups been quick to defend the rights of polygamists.

For our present society to single out Mormon polygamy for special legal censure strikes me as profoundly hypocritical.

For what it is worth, I want to offer a modest defense of the right to practice polygamy in our pluralistic society. Let me make it clear right off, however, that I do not believe that polygamy is a good thing. It goes against some of my deepest evangelical convictions about marriage and family life. As I read the New Testament, monogamy is the pattern that God has willed for the marital relationship. To put it bluntly, I believe that polygamy is sinful. But I also believe that not everything that is sinful should be viewed as illegal. In our pluralistic society, where people of various worldviews and value systems are attempting to live together with some semblance of harmony, we need to tolerate many things we consider morally wrong. We should only legislate against those practices that pose serious threats to the fundamental rights of other human beings. This means, as I see things, that we ought to go out of our way to tolerate practices based on the sincerely held convictions of people with whom we disagree.

For example, I believe that Jehovah's Witnesses are wrong to refuse blood tranfusions, but I want to respect their views on the subject. I do favor having the state declare the child of a Jehovah's Witness family a temporary ward of the court when a blood tranfusion is necessary to save the child's life. But even in such extreme cases, I regret the need to violate sincerely held convictions.

Banning Polygamy Is Hypocritical

My bias, then, is in favor of the Mormon polygamists—unless, of course, it can be demonstrated that their marital practices are a significant threat to the social fabric. And while I do want to take seriously the reports of spouse abuse in those settings, I think we can deal with that problem without simply banning all plural marriages. I also take reports of spouse abuse seriously in *monogamous* marriages, but this certainly doesn't lead me to oppose monogamy as such.

Actually, for our present society to single out Mormon polygamy for special legal censure strikes me as profoundly hypocritical. Think of related practices we do not treat as criminal. "Serial monogamy" is a long-established pattern in contemporary life; many popular leaders in our culture have gone through multiple marriages and divorces, sharing parental responsibilities with a variety of former partners. In some urban subcultures, teenage males have fathered children with several different single mothers, often without acknowledging any serious sense of parental obligation. And none of this is illegal. Indeed, the promiscuous behavior of many well-known folks in the entertainment business is itself the stuff of our own entertainment.

In comparison with these other departures from the norms of monogamous family life, Mormon plural marriages—for all my disagreement with the religious and moral assumptions they take for granted—manifest some values I admire. There is at least an emphasis on stable community and a commitment to hands-on parenting.

I have never talked to a Mormon polygamist, nor do I have any inclination to do so. But my hunch is that if I ever were to engage in such a conversation, I would not be nearly as irritated as I have been when talking to people—as I often do—who seem to make light of their commitments as spouses and parents. In these latter conversations, I often express my disagreements with such folks with considerable passion. But I have never thought to have them thrown in jail because of what I take to be their irresponsible patterns of behavior. I see no reason why I should be harsher with Mormon practitioners of plural marriage.

2

Polygamists Should Be Prosecuted

Suzan Mazur

Suzan Mazur is a journalist who has published articles in News-day, *the* Philadelphia Inquirer, Maclean's, *and* Scoop.

While HBO's series Big Love *may be entertaining, it fails to explore serious issues of abuse within polygamous communities. Even federal and state authorities have overlooked these abuses (rape, child abuse, and drug addiction) for the past decade. Polygamist cults are scattered in various locations in the western United States and along the Canadian border, though overall, polygamy as a lifestyle may be on the decline. Still, organizations like the American Civil Liberties Union continue to support the right of plural marriages, and television programs like* Big Love *glamorize polygamy. What truly is needed are leaders who are willing to prosecute these illegal polygamous colonies.*

Polygamy, American style. That's the theme of the new HBO series *Big Love*, all about a polygamist family in Utah. *Big Love*'s executive producer is Tom Hanks, who spent a couple of his childhood years in the Mormon church. The show passes very lightly over issues of rape, child abuse, and drug addiction arising in polygamist enclaves.

Despite serious, front-page media coverage for most of the last decade, such human-rights abuses are going on right now in polygamist settlements throughout the country. The Department of Homeland Security knows about it. So does the

FBI and the Bush administration. Polygamy continues, if not with the active assistance of government and law enforcement, then certainly with their indolence and incompetence.

The U.S. Department of Justice has failed to dismantle the best-documented polygamy cults. The epicenter is well-known: the towns of Hildale, Utah, and Colorado City, Arizona, both dominated by the extremist and secretive branch of Mormonism known as the Fundamentalist Church of Latter Day Saints, or FLDS. These towns are satirized in the encampment named "Jupiter Creek" in *Big Love.*

The government instead is now singling out one polygamy "prophet"—FLDS leader Warren Jeffs, with the FBI offering $50,000 for information leading to his arrest for sexual assault of a minor. Jeffs, who has not been seen for four years, has built yet another polygamy compound near Custer, South Dakota, adding to existing sites on the Utah-Arizona strip; in Eldorado, Texas; and straddling either side of the Idaho-British Columbia border. In these compounds, women allegedly have been drugged, brainwashed, and repeatedly impregnated until they are physically and emotionally wasted. Teenage boys allegedly are tossed out into the world without any real education so that the ratio of males to females in the cult remains favorable to the alpha males.

Polygamous Cults

Polygamy cults are scattered up and down the Rocky Mountains from British Columbia to the Mexican border. Yet however many there are, they clearly remain an aberration on the American landscape. Experts estimate total U.S. polygamists at only 100,000, with Utah home to an estimated 30,000 to 50,000 practitioners. Fundamentalist Mormon polygamists include the Kingstons—numbering about 1,500—who have prospered from investments in the gaming business, and 8,000 to 10,000 Allreds, who live just outside Salt Lake City, in Nevada, and in Pinesdale, Montana. The Blackmore branch of the FLDS is in the logging business on either side of the Idaho-British Columbia border.

Utah's attorney general, Mark Shurtleff, like federal authorities, has chosen to nibble around the edges of the problem—investigating individual domestic-violence complaints, but failing to identify the whole polygamy enterprise itself as domestic violence.

Shurtleff says he is strapped for money, and he warns of the economic consequences of breaking up the cults. But it is clear that the political and economic power of the FLDS so far has prevented the cults' further undoing.

Among non-Mormon cultists there is The Family, organized in the 1960s by David Berg and long scrutinized for sexual practices including pedophilia, incest, and rape. Less known is The House of Yahweh, an Old Testament sect led by former Abilene, Texas, police officer Yisrayl "Buffalo Bill" Hawkins, with 2,500 followers based in Abilene and scattered (many in trailers) through at least a dozen states. Yahweh cultists say no Scriptures forbid plural wives as sin.

Is Polygamy Growing?

Is polygamy a growing phenomenon? Probably not, though it is hard to know. Some cults have their own midwives and hospitals, police, judges, and school superintendents. Birth and death records are not reliable, as evidenced by an entire cemetery of unmarked baby graves—"Babyland"—attached to an FLDS cult on the Utah-Arizona border.

Nor is the momentum in the direction of legalization, not even in Utah. My impression, from having studied U.S. polygamy for the best part of a decade, is that significant numbers are leaving the lifestyle.

One polygamist judge, Walter Steed, was recently removed from the bench by the Utah Supreme Court for flouting the state's law against bigamy [marrying a person when already married to another person]. Activists from Tapestry Against Polygamy—former "plural wives"—filed a complaint with the Judicial Conduct Commission to unseat Steed, who had heard cases for a quarter of a century. Tapestry Against Polygamy also helped raise Utah's marriage age.

With the evidence piling up of harm done to women and children within this world, what is truly amazing is that it still exists.

Who Will Take Legal Action?

Still, there is *Big Love*. And there is also American Civil Liberties Union (ACLU) president Nadine Strossen, quoted as saying in a speech at Yale that the ACLU has defended the rights of individuals to engage in polygamy. Some interpret this as an ACLU endorsement and link it to the ACLU's protection of gay rights.

But commentators such as Charles Krauthammer, who worry about the decriminalization of polygamy, protest too much. It's the antipolygamy activists, like Andrea Emmett, author of *God's Brothel* and an outgoing president of the National Organization of Women chapter in Salt Lake City, who are on the growing, sane side of the issue. She describes polygamy as the "biggest threat to the women and children of Utah."

Rowenna Erickson, a former Kingston wife and cofounder of Tapestry Against Polygamy, says she does not think polygamy will ever be decriminalized in the United States: "They've been trying to lump polygamy with gays and lesbians forever."

So this, if you can even call it a "movement," is a sensational but very small one, linked with extremist beliefs of one kind or another. We don't really need a cartoonish TV series glamorizing it. With the evidence piling up of harm done to women and children within this world, what is truly amazing is that it still exists. What we really need are courageous local and national leaders who will face down local powers and show polygamy some Big Law.

3

North Americans Should Be Free to Choose Polygamy

Karen Selick

Karen Selick is a lawyer in Belleville, Ontario.

In recent years, a large polygamous community has established itself in Bountiful, British Columbia. While both Christians and feminists have criticized the community for exploiting women, women within the community have stated that they have freely chosen, and even enjoy, the lifestyle. Although accusations of pedophilia and forced marriages leveled against the community are disturbing, these alleged practices have no connection with polygamy per se; these activities are already illegal, whatever one's practicing religion. The practice of polygamy has a long history, and while many condemn the practice, they should nonetheless allow citizens within free societies a choice of religious practice.

It's perfectly legal in Canada for an adult who lives alone to have sexual relations with a different partner every day of the week. Something else that's perfectly legal is for a group of celibate adults to reside in a house together—sharing the chores, sharing their meals, and even pooling their finances if they wish.

What's not legal is trying to combine the two—having your multiple sex partners move in so that you can share the joy of sex as well as the joy of cooking in the comfort of your mutual household. Do that, and you could find yourself charged with polygamy under section 293 of the Criminal Code.

Karen Selick, "Polygamy—Two Rights Shouldn't Make a Wrong," *karenselick.com*, 2005. Reproduced by permission of the author.

Prosecutions for polygamy seem to have been very rare in Canada. The only reported case I could find was from 1937. This may change in the near future. The community of Bountiful, British Columbia, has been making headlines recently over allegations that a group of breakaways from the Mormon church are practicing polygamy.

Talk about strange bedfellows! Both feminist groups and mainstream Christian groups, not known for seeing eye to eye very often, are lobbying for the British Columbia government to press charges.

What Is So Bad About Polygamy?

Although sharing a husband with another woman wouldn't be my cup of tea, I don't understand why our lawmakers insist that polygamy be outlawed. Some of the Bountiful women declare unambiguously that they enjoy their way of life, that they are there voluntarily, and that they don't want their "plural marriages" broken up by criminal charges. They cite the sharing of household chores and the caring relationship with their cowives as among the advantages.

While legal polygamy seems unthinkable to most Canadians today, it actually has a very long history.

Is it not conceivable that these are fully informed, psychologically healthy individuals, free from duress and telling the truth? If so, that would mean that polygamy is in their case a victimless crime—a mere offence against state fiat, rather than a violation of their rights or anyone else's.

Those campaigning for prosecution allege there is more sinister behavior in Bountiful. "It's basically incest and pedophilia that's going on there, in our opinion" says Jancis Andrews, an activist urging prosecution.

Those are troubling allegations. But pedophilia is a crime in its own right. So is holding someone against her will. So is

intimidating or threatening someone. So is fraudulently marrying a second spouse when you've lied and led her to believe
you weren't already married. These are all crimes that have
genuine victims, that is, persons who don't want done to them
what is being done, or who are too young to legally consent to
what is being done. If such crimes are occurring, the answer is
simple: we should prosecute for them. But we shouldn't out-
law something that in many cases is a consensual, victimless
activity on the mere off-chance that it will make it more convenient to catch people who are committing different crimes.

Polygamy's Long History

While legal polygamy seems unthinkable to most Canadians
today, it actually has a very long history. Economist Theodore
C. Bergstrom, in his paper "On the Economics of Polygyny,"
says: "Of 1170 societies recorded in Murdock's *Ethnographic
Atlas*, polygyny (some men having more than one wife) is
prevalent in 850." Polygamy was not outlawed in the United
States until 1862.

The bible is full of prominent figures who had multiple
wives: Abraham, Jacob, David, and Solomon, to name a few.
One Catholic with whom I debated this point told me these
cases were God's way of "warning us by example" that polygamy "doesn't work". However, if the existence of domestic
discord among biblical polygamists speaks poorly for polygamy, what does today's rampant divorce rate say about the
wisdom of monogamy?

Ironically, when the legal challenge to the constitutionality
of Canada's antipolygamy law does come, it will probably not
come on the grounds of liberty or privacy, but on the grounds
of religious freedom. The Bountiful group, members of the
Fundamentalist Church of Jesus Christ of Latter Day Saints
(FLDS), say polygamy is an important tenet of their religion.
Outlawing it is tantamount to forbidding them the freedom to
practice their faith. Earlier this year [2005], an American po-

lygamist urged Utah's Supreme Court to strike down the polygamy ban as an unconstitutional violation of religious freedom. That decision is still pending as I write this. [The Court upheld the ban.]

Give people the freedom to choose and let's see what happens.

Religious Freedom and Polygamy

The Muslim religion also permits polygamy. *Western Standard* magazine recently reported that one Islamic group in Vancouver cites the legalization of polygamy as "one of [the] group's long-term goals." The 1998 case of *Ali v. Canada (Minister of Citizenship and Immigration)* held that an immigration officer had rightly refused Mr. Ali's application for permanent residence because he had two legal Kuwaiti marriages and planned to bring both his wives with him to Canada. It's not hard to imagine that future rulings of this kind might be appealed on the grounds of religious freedom.

What irritates me is the people who are absolutely positive that their way is the best way, but who are afraid to put it to the test. Give people the freedom to choose and let's see what happens. If mainstream Christians are right that monogamy is superior to polygamy, simply let the two systems operate side-by-side and watch all the Muslims be won over. If you're not prepared to allow that test, doesn't it suggest that you harbor uncertainty about the superiority of your own system?

4

Polygamy Limits Freedom of Choice

Anonymous, as told to Sana Butler

The person featured in this article grew up and eventually escaped from her polygamous community.

Within the Fundamental Church of Jesus Christ of Latter Day Saints, parents and church leaders control a young girl's life. At 16, young girls are sometimes married to men much older who practice polygamy. Within the community, girls are taught very little about the outside world in school, and questioning the Mormon faith can lead to punishment. Even when a young girl escapes from the community, the outside world provides little protection: although polygamy is illegal, children cannot be removed from a household unless the parents are considered unfit. The only option for some children is to remain in hiding.

Hildale, Utah, where I lived my whole life, until recently, is a pretty regular town. There's a zoo, a few parks, a local Wal-mart. At night, you can see all the stars. But it's different in the way that people do things.

Most of Hildale's 1,800 residents, including my family, belong to the Fundamentalist Church of Jesus Christ of Latter Day Saints. Our church, which is not recognized as a branch of Mormonism, dictates that girls can be married soon after their sixteenth birthdays to men who are often 30 or 40 years older and already have a number of wives. According to our church, a man can't make it to the highest degree of Heaven if he has fewer than three wives. The number of wives the church grants a man is based on how faithful he and his family are, or how valuable his land is. Single-wife families are outcasts.

Family and Community Life

My father says that it's an honor to have more than one wife, but he hasn't been given another yet. I don't think my mom could have a second woman in the house, although we never talked about it. My parents have fourteen kids. A woman is supposed to have as many as she can until she's physically worn out. The typical family has four wives and 20 children, but I know one with 25 wives and 300 kids.

Our community is led by a man named Warren Jeffs. He calls himself a prophet of God. You need Warren's permission to do anything, including taking a vacation. Just tell him where and when, and he'll go with you. According to our church, the laws of Warren are more important than those of the American government, since his represent the word of God. So if he told you to go break a law, you'd do it.

I began to realize that despite what I was taught, the outside world is not evil.

School consists of classes in religion, sewing, and cooking. I never learned about science or history. I didn't even know the name of the U.S. president. We were taught that Warren was the president. Warren keeps a list of girls whose fathers have turned them in to be married. My dad submitted my name when I was fourteen, which meant that as soon as I turned sixteen, I could be married, and Warren could choose the man. I remember telling my father that I didn't want to be someone's seventeenth wife. He said, But it's your religion. And I said, But it's my life. He called me ungrateful and sent me to bed.

Questioning Mormon Faith

After that, I started rebelling: going out at night, talking to boys. I listened to public radio, which was also forbidden. I began to realize that despite what I was taught, the outside world is not evil. I became friends with another girl who expressed doubts about our church. Her name was Fawn. But perhaps the biggest wake-up call was when my oldest brother left. Before he ran he said, Listen to what your heart is saying.

A female runaway faces greater danger than a male runaway.

One day, Fawn asked if I ever thought about the world beyond Hildale. I told her that I didn't think I had enough courage to leave. A female runaway faces greater danger than a male runaway. Men are sent to bring you back, at which point either your future husband or your father beats you so badly that you never run again.

Then in January, Warren announced that 20 men in our town had sinned, and were no longer worthy of their families. Their wives and children would be reassigned to different husbands. Meanwhile, the rest of the community would be forced to fast as part of the sinners' penance.

I wasn't buying it. I opened the fridge and took out an apple. My father screamed at me to spit it out. I told him, I'm sorry if this hurts your feelings, but I am not going without food for Warren Jeffs. And actually, I think this world would be better off without him. I tried to sound confident, but I was shaking. He slapped me and sent me to my room, and warned me that the outside world was a dangerous place. If I ever left, I'd probably get beaten or raped. I called Fawn. It was now or never. Fawn's boyfriend picked us up and brought us to a friend of his mom's who could help us. That friend gave us the number for a group called Tapestry Against Polygamy. Tapestry put us in contact with a woman named Flora

Jessop, who had fled from our town years ago. I'd heard about Flora all my life, that she was a home wrecker who helped girls escape forced marriages. She picked us up an hour later, wearing leather pants and a matching jacket. She looked like Superwoman to me. Flora brought us to a friend's house and notified Child Protective Services. But apparently, raising us in polygamist homes, though illegal, did not deem our parents unfit. Since we were under eighteen, we'd be required to return home. There was nothing left to do but run. Fawn and I are still in hiding. Her older brother, who also left Hildale, wants to assume temporary custody of us, and right now we're trying to make it work. My parents have already given their okays. They're very disappointed, but at least this way they know I'll be safe. I call my mom a lot to tell her that I'm fine. She can't say it, but I believe that she wanted me to have a regular life. Unfortunately, my father rules the house.

I tell my mom that what we're taught about life outside Hildale is wrong. I wish she could see what it's like for herself. I think she'd like it.

5

Non-Monogamous Relationships Lead to Jealousy

William Saletan

William Saletan is Slate's *national correspondent and author of* Bearing Right: How Conservatives Won the Abortion War.

In an attempt to convince the public that gay marriage is a dangerous precedent, conservatives have argued that gay marriage will lead to the legalization of polygamy. The argument, however, leaves out a fundamental aspect of human nature: jealously. Even people who willingly enter into polygamous or polyamorist (multiple unmarried partners) relationships frequently founder on jealous feelings. When looking at biblical history, the Ten Commandments addressed God's jealousy, and the polygamous practices of early patriarchs (Abraham, David, and Solomon) frequently led to discord. Polygamy is an outmoded practice that has never benefited the people involved and has nothing in common with gay marriage.

Uh-oh. Conservatives are starting to hyperventilate again. You know the symptoms: In a haystack of right-wing dominance, they find a needle of radicalism, declare it a mortal danger to civilization, and use it to rally their voters in the next election. First it was flag-burning. Then it was the "war on Christmas." Now it's polygamy. Having crushed gay marriage nationwide in 2004, they need to gin up a new threat to the family. They've found it in *Big Love*, the HBO series about a guy with three wives. Open the door to gay marriage, they warn, and group marriage will be next.

William Saletan, "Don't Do Unto Others: The Difference Between Gay Marriage and Polygamy," *Slate.com*, March 23, 2006. Distributed by United Feature Syndicate, Inc. Available at www.slate.com/id/2138482.

My friend Charles Krauthammer makes the argument succinctly in the *Washington Post*. "Traditional marriage is defined as the union of (1) two people of (2) opposite gender," he observes. "If, as advocates of gay marriage insist, the gender requirement is nothing but prejudice, exclusion and an arbitrary denial of one's autonomous choices," then "on what grounds do they insist upon the traditional, arbitrary, and exclusionary number of two?"

Here's the answer. The number isn't two. It's one. You commit to one person, and that person commits wholly to you. Second, the number isn't arbitrary. It's based on human nature. Specifically, on jealousy.

Jealousy and Polygamy

In an excellent *Weekly Standard* article against gay marriage and polygamy, Stanley Kurtz of the Hudson Institute discusses several recent polygamous unions. In one case, "two wives agreed to allow their husbands to establish a public and steady sexual relationship." Unfortunately, "one of the wives remains uncomfortable with this arrangement," so "the story ends with at least the prospect of one marriage breaking up." In another case, "two bisexual-leaning men meet a woman and create a threesome that produces two children, one by each man." Same result: "the trio's eventual breakup."

Look up other articles on polygamy, even sympathetic ones, and you'll see the pattern. A Columbia News Service report on last month's national conference of polyamorists—people who love, but don't necessarily marry, multiple partners—features Robyn Trask, the managing editor of a magazine called *Loving More*. The conference Web site says she "has been practicing polyamory for 16 years." But according to the article, "When Trask confronted her husband about sneaking around with a long-distance girlfriend for three months, he denied it. . . . The couple is now separated and plans to divorce." A *Houston Press* article on another couple describes how "John and Brianna opened up their relationship to another woman," but "it ended badly, with the woman throwing dishes." Now they're in another threesome. "I do get jealous at times," John tells the reporter. "But not to the point where I can't flip it off."

Fidelity isn't natural, but jealousy is.

Good luck, John. I'm sure polyamorists are right that lots of people "find joy in having close relationships . . . with multiple partners." The average guy would love to bang his neighbor's wife. He just doesn't want his wife banging his neighbor. Fidelity isn't natural, but jealousy is. Hence the one-spouse rule. One isn't the number of people you want to sleep with. It's the number of people you want your spouse to sleep with.

Polygamy's Long History

We've been this way for a long time. Look at the Ten Commandments. One: "Thou shalt have no other gods before me." Two: "Thou shalt not make unto thee any graven image. . . . Thou shalt not bow down thyself to them, nor serve them: for I the Lord thy God am a jealous God." Three: "Thou shalt not take the name of the Lord thy God in vain." In case the message isn't clear enough, the list proceeds to "Thou shalt not commit adultery" and "shalt not covet thy neighbor's wife."

Some people say the Bible sanctions polygamy. "Abraham, David, Jacob, and Solomon were all favored by God and were all polygamists," argues law professor Jonathan Turley. Favored? Look what polygamy did for them. Sarah told Abraham to sleep with her servant. When the servant got pregnant and came to despise Sarah, Sarah kicked her out. Rachel and Leah fought over Jacob, who ended up stripping his eldest son of his birthright for sleeping with Jacob's concubine. David got rid of Bathsheba's husband by ordering troops to betray him in battle. Promiscuity had the first word, but jealousy always had the last.

Thousands of years later, we've changed our ideas about slavery, patriarchy, and homosexuality. But we're still jealous.

Thousands of years later, we've changed our ideas about slavery, patriarchy, and homosexuality. But we're still jealous. While 21 percent of married or divorced Americans admit to having cheated (and surveys suggest husbands are more likely than wives to stray emotionally and physically), only one in four women says she'd give a cheating husband or boyfriend a second chance, and only 5 to 6 percent of adults consider polygamy or extramarital affairs morally acceptable. As the above cases show, even people who try to practice polygamy struggle with feelings of betrayal.

Polygamous Practices Are Out of Date

Krauthammer finds the gay/poly divergence perplexing. "Polygamy was sanctioned, indeed common" for ages, he observes. "What is historically odd is that as gay marriage is gaining acceptance, the resistance to polygamy is much more powerful." But when you factor in jealousy, the oddity disappears. Women shared husbands because they had to. The alternative was poverty. As women gained power, they began to choose what they really wanted. And what they really wanted was the same fidelity that men expected from them.

Gays who seek to marry want the same thing. They're not looking for the right to sleep around. They already have that. It's called dating. A friend once explained to me why gay men have sex on the first date: Nobody says no. Your partner, being of the same sex, is as eager as you are to get it on. But he's also as eager as you are to get it on with somebody else. And if you really like him, you don't want that. You want him all to yourself. That's why marriage, not polygamy, is in your nature, and in our future.

6

Jealousy in Non-Monogamous Relationships Can Be Overcome

Jorge N. Ferrer

Jorge N. Ferrer is associate professor of East-West psychology at the California Institute of Integral Studies, San Francisco.

Sympathetic joy for the happiness of other people, commonly experienced in intimate partnerships, allows individuals to overcome selfishness and gain a broader view of the world. This joy, however, often turns to jealousy when one's partner experiences it with someone else. Many people assume that jealousy is a more basic emotion than sympathetic joy, but what if that jealousy could be transformed into compassion? This would allow individuals to grow emotionally beyond monogamy, leaving possessive jealousy behind. Many object to this possibility, arguing that non-monogamy destroys relationships. But monogamy, as it is now practiced in the West, often masks polyamory (multiple intimate relationships). Increasingly, couples marry multiple times and many commit adultery. Allowing for multiple intimate relationships would erase the duplicity of adultery and the boredom that many experience in monogamous relationships, allowing one to grow emotionally and spiritually with other people. Western culture's commitment to monogamy actually may be causing more pain than emotional satisfaction.

In Buddhism, sympathetic joy (*mudita*) is regarded as one of the "four immeasurable states" (*brahmaviharas*) or qualities of an enlightened person—the other three being loving kindness (*metta*), compassion (*karuna*), and equanimity (*upeksha*). Sympathetic joy refers to the human capability to participate in the joy of others, to feel happy when others feel happy. Although with different emphases, such understanding can also be found in the contemplative teachings of many other religious traditions such as the Kabbalah, Christianity, or Sufism, which in their respective languages talk about empathic joy, for example, in terms of opening the "eye of the heart." According to these and other traditions, the cultivation of sympathetic joy can break through the ultimately false duality between self and others, being therefore a potent aid on the path toward overcoming self-centeredness and achieving liberation.

Most psychologically balanced individuals naturally share, to some degree, in the happiness of their mates.

Though the ultimate aim of many religious practices is to develop sympathetic joy for all sentient beings, intimate relationships offer human beings—whether they are spiritual practitioners or not—a precious opportunity to taste its experiential flavor. Most psychologically balanced individuals naturally share, to some degree, in the happiness of their mates. Bliss and delight can effortlessly emerge within us as we feel the joy of our partner's ecstatic dance, enjoyment of an art performance, relishing of a favorite dish, or serene contemplation of a splendid sunset. And this innate capacity for sympathetic joy in intimate relationships often reaches its peak in deeply emotional shared experiences, sensual exchange, and lovemaking. When we are in love, the embodied joy of our beloved becomes extremely contagious.

Jealousy in Monogamous Relationships

But what if our partner's sensuous or emotional joy were to arise in relation not to us but to someone else? For the vast majority of people, the immediate reaction would likely be not one of expansive openness and love, but rather of contracting fear, anger, and perhaps even violent rage. The change of a single variable has rapidly turned the selfless contentment of sympathetic joy into the "green-eyed monster" of jealousy, as Shakespeare called this compulsive emotion.

Perhaps due to its prevalence, jealousy is widely accepted as "normal" in most cultures, and many of its violent consequences have often been regarded as understandable, morally justified, and even legally permissible. (It is worth remembering that as late as the 1970s the law of states such as Texas, Utah, and New Mexico considered "reasonable" the homicide of one's adulterous partner if it happened at the scene of discovery!) Though there are circumstances in which the mindful expression of rightful anger (not violence) may be a temporary appropriate response—for example, in the case of the adulterous breaking of monogamous vows—jealousy frequently makes its appearance in interpersonal situations where no betrayal has taken place or when we rationally know that no real threat actually exists (for example, watching our partner's sensuous dance with an attractive person at a party). In general, the awakening of sympathetic joy in observing the happiness of one's mate in relationship with perceived "rivals" is an extremely rare pearl to find. In the context of romantic relationships, jealousy functions as a hindrance to sympathetic joy. . . .

Transforming Jealousy into Sympathetic Joy

To my knowledge, in contrast to most other emotional states, jealousy has no antonym in any human language. This is probably why the Kerista community—a San Francisco-based polygamous group that was disbanded in the early 1990s—

coined the term "compersion" to refer to the emotional response opposite to jealousy. The Keristas defined compersion as "the feeling of taking joy in the joy that others you love share among themselves." Since the term emerged in the context of the practice of "polyfidelity" (faithfulness to many), it encompassed sensuous and sexual joy, but compersion was only cultivated when a person had loving bonds with all parties involved. However, the feeling of compersion can also be extended to any situation in which our mate feels emotional/sensuous joy with others in wholesome and constructive ways. In these situations, we can rejoice in our partner's joy even if we do not know the third parties. Experientially, compersion can be felt as a tangible presence in the heart whose awakening may be accompanied by waves of warmth, pleasure, and appreciation at the idea of our partner loving others and being loved by them in nonharmful and mutually beneficial ways. In this light, I suggest that compersion can be seen as a novel extension of sympathetic joy in the realm of intimate relationships, and particularly in interpersonal situations that conventionally evoke feelings of jealousy. . . .

Let us explore now the implications of transforming jealousy in our intimate relationships. I suggest that the transformation of jealousy through the cultivation of sympathetic joy bolsters the awakening of the enlightened heart. As jealousy dissolves, universal compassion and unconditional love become more easily available to the individual. Human compassion is universal in its embrace of all sentient beings without qualifications. Human love is also all-inclusive and unconditional—a love that is both free from the tendency to possess and that does not expect anything in return. Although to love without conditions is generally easier in the case of brotherly and spiritual love, I suggest that as we heal the historical split between spiritual love (*agape*) and sensuous love (*eros*), the extension of sympathetic joy to more embodied forms of love becomes a natural development. And when embodied love is emancipated from possessiveness, a richer range of spiritually legitimate relationship options organically emerges. As people become more whole and are freed from certain basic fears (e.g., of abandonment, unworthiness, or engulfment), new possibilities for the expression of embodied love open up, which may feel natural, safe, and wholesome, rather than undesirable, threatening, or even morally questionable. For example, once jealousy turns into sympathetic joy, and sensuous and spiritual love are integrated, a couple may feel drawn to extend their love to other individuals beyond the structure of the pair bond. In short, once jealousy loosens its grip on the contemporary self, human love can attain a wider dimension of embodiment in our lives that may naturally lead to the mindful cultivation of more inclusive intimate connections.

Social monogamy frequently masks biological polyamory in an increasingly significant number of couples.

Social Monogamy as a Mask for Biological Polyamory (Multiple Intimate Relationships)

Even if mindful and open, the inclusion of other loving connections in the context of a partnership can elicit the two classic objections to non-monogamy (or polyamory): First, it does not work in practice; and second, it leads to the destruction of relationships. (I am leaving aside here the deeply engrained moral opposition to the very idea of polyamory associated with the legacy of Christianity in the West.) As for the first objection, though polygyny ("many wives") is still culturally prevalent on the globe—out of 853 known human cultures, 84 percent permit polygyny—it seems undeniable that with a few exceptions, modern attempts at more gender-egalitarian and open relationships have not been very successful. Nevertheless, the same could be said about monogamy. After all, the history of monogamy is the history of adultery. As [British author] H.H. Munro wrote, monogamy is "the

Western custom of one wife and hardly any mistresses." Summing up the available evidence, David Buss [psychologist] estimates that "approximately 20 to 40 percent of American women and 30 to 50 percent of American men have at least one affair over the course of their marriage," and recent surveys suggest that the chance of either member of a modern couple committing infidelity at some point in their marriage may be as high as 76 percent—with these numbers increasing every year. Though most people in our culture consider themselves—and are believed to be—monogamous, anonymous surveys reveal that many are so socially, but not biologically.

In other words, social monogamy frequently masks biological polyamory in an increasingly significant number of couples. In her book *Anatomy of Love*, prominent anthropologist Helen Fisher suggests that the human desire for clandestine extramarital sex is genetically grounded in the evolutionary advantages that having other mates provided for both genders in ancestral times: extra opportunities to spread DNA for males, and extra protection and resources, plus the acquisition of potentially better sperm for females. It may also be important to note that the prevalent relationship paradigm in the modern West is no longer lifelong monogamy ("till death do us part"), but serial monogamy (many partners sequentially), often punctuated with adultery. Serial monogamy, plus clandestine adultery, is in many respects not too different from polyamory, except perhaps in that the latter is more honest, ethical, and arguably less harmful. In this context, the mindful exploration of polyamory may help in alleviating the suffering caused by the staggering number of clandestine affairs in our modern culture.

Furthermore, to disregard a potentially emancipatory cultural development because its early manifestations did not succeed may be unwise. Looking back at the history of emancipatory movements in the West—from feminism to the abolition of slavery to the gaining of civil rights by African Americans—we can see that the first waves of the Promethean impulse were frequently burdened with problems and distortions, which only later could be recognized and resolved. This is not the place to review this historical evidence, but to dismiss polyamory because of its previous failures may be equivalent to having written off feminism on the grounds that its first waves failed to reclaim genuine feminine values or free women from patriarchy (e.g., turning women into masculinized "superwomen" capable of succeeding in a patriarchal world).

A Path Toward Emotional and Spiritual Depth

But wait a moment. Dyadic [two units regarded as one; a pair] relationships are already challenging enough. Why complicate them further by adding extra parties to the equation? From a spiritual standpoint, an intimate relationship can be viewed as a structure through which human beings can learn to express and receive love in many forms. Although I would hesitate to declare polyamory more spiritual or evolved than monogamy, it is clear that if a person has not mastered the lessons and challenges of the dyadic structure, he or she may not be ready to take on the challenges of more complex forms of relationships. Therefore, the objection of impracticability may be valid in many cases.

The second common objection to polyamory is that it results in the dissolution of pair bonds. The rationale is that the intimate contact with others will increase the chances that one member of the couple will abandon the other and run off with a more appealing mate. This concern is understandable, but the fact is that people are having affairs, falling in love, and leaving their partners all the time in the context of monogamous vows. As we have seen, adultery goes hand in hand with monogamy, and lifelong monogamy has been mostly replaced with serial monogamy (or sequential polyamory) in our culture. Parenthetically, vows of lifelong monogamy create often unrealistic expectations that add suffering to the pain involved in the termination of any relationship—and one could also raise questions about the wholesomeness of the psychological needs for certainty and security that such vows normally meet. In any event, although it may sound counter-intuitive at first, the threat of abandonment may be actually reduced in polyamory, since the loving bond that our partner may develop with another person does not necessarily mean that he or she must choose between them or us (or lie to us).

Human beings are endowed with widely diverse biological, psychological, and spiritual dispositions that predispose them toward different relationship styles.

More positively, the new qualities and passions that novel intimate connections can awaken within a person can also bring a renewed sense of creative dynamism to the sexual/emotional life of the couple, whose frequent stagnation after three or four years (seven in some cases) is the chief cause of clandestine affairs and separation. As recent surveys show, the number of couples who successfully navigate the so-called four- and seven-year itches is decreasing every year. Mindful polyamory (i.e., practiced with the full knowledge and approval of all concerned) may also offer an alternative to the usually unfulfilling nature of currently prevalent serial monogamy in which people change partners every few years, never benefiting from the emotional and spiritual depth that only an enduring connection with another human being provides. In a context of psychospiritual growth, such exploration can create unique opportunities for the development of emotional maturity, the transmutation of jealousy into sympathetic joy, the emancipation of embodied love from exclusivity and possessiveness, and the integration of sensuous and spiritual love. As Christian mystic Richard of St. Victor maintains, mature love between lover and beloved naturally reaches beyond itself toward a third reality, and this opening, I suggest, might in some cases be crucial both to overcome codependent tendencies and to foster the health, creative vitality, and perhaps even longevity of intimate relationships.

The culturally prevalent belief ... that the only spiritually correct sexual options are either celibacy or monogamy is a myth that may be causing unnecessary suffering.

I should stress that my intent is not to argue for the superiority of any relationship style over others—a discussion I find both pointless and misleading. Human beings are endowed with widely diverse biological, psychological, and spiritual dispositions that predispose them toward different relationship styles: celibacy, monogamy, serial monogamy, or polyamory. In other words, many equally valid psychospiritual trajectories may call individuals to engage in one or another relationship style either for life or at specific junctures in their paths. Whereas the psychospiritual foundation for this diversity of mating responses cannot be empirically established, recent discoveries in neuroscience support the idea of a genetic base. When scientists inserted a piece of DNA from a monogamous species of mice (prairie voles) into males from a different—and highly promiscuous—mice species, the latter turned fervently monogamous. What is more striking is that some people carry an extra bit of DNA in a gene responsible for the distribution of vasopressin receptors in the brain (a hormone associated with attachment bonds), while others do not, and that piece of DNA is very similar to the one found in the monogamous prairie voles. Although the implications of this finding for our understanding of human mating await further clarification, it strongly suggests that a diversity of relationship styles—both monogamous and polyamorous—may be genetically imprinted in humans. . . .

Beyond Monogamy and Polyamory

It is my hope that this essay opens avenues for dialogue and inquiry in spiritual circles about the transformation of intimate relationships. It is also my hope that it contributes to the extension of spiritual virtues, such as sympathetic joy, to all areas of life and in particular to those which, due to historical, cultural, and perhaps evolutionary reasons, have been traditionally excluded or overlooked—areas such as sexuality and romantic love.

The culturally prevalent belief—supported by many contemporary spiritual teachers—that the only spiritually correct sexual options are either celibacy or monogamy is a myth that may be causing unnecessary suffering and that needs, therefore, to be laid to rest. It may be perfectly plausible to hold simultaneously more than one loving or sexual bond in a context of mindfulness, ethical integrity, and spiritual growth, for example, while working toward the transformation of jealousy into sympathetic joy and the integration of sensuous and spiritual love. I should add right away that, ultimately, I believe that the greatest expression of spiritual freedom in intimate relationships does not lie in strictly sticking to any particular relationship style—whether monogamous or polyamorous—but rather in a radical openness to the dynamic unfolding of life that eludes any fixed or predetermined structure of relationships. It should be obvious, for example, that one can follow a specific relationship style for the "right" (e.g., life-enhancing) or "wrong" (e.g., fear-based) reasons; that all relationship styles can become equally limiting spiritual ideologies; and that different internal and external conditions may rightfully call us to engage in different relationship styles at various junctures of our lives. It is in this open space catalyzed by the movement beyond monogamy and polyamory,

I believe, that an existential stance deeply attuned to the standpoint of Spirit can truly emerge.

Nevertheless, gaining awareness about the ancestral—and mostly obsolete—nature of the evolutionary impulses that direct our sexual/emotional responses and relationship choices may empower us to consciously co-create a future in which expanded forms of spiritual freedom may have a greater chance to bloom. Who knows, perhaps as we extend spiritual practice to intimate relationships, new petals of liberation will blossom that may not only emancipate our minds, hearts, and consciousness, but also our bodies and instinctive world. Can we envision an "integral bodhisattva [enlightened existence] vow" in which the conscious mind renounces full liberation until the body and the primary world can be free as well?

7

Same-Sex Marriage Opens the Door for Legalizing Polygamy

Stanley Kurtz

Stanley Kurtz is an adjunct fellow of the Hudson Institute and a fellow at the Hoover Institution.

The legalization of gay marriage will lead to the legalization of polygamy and eventually the end of marriage as an institution. Simply put, polygamy is incompatible with companionate marriages. Nontraditional marriages that operate outside of religious traditions are unbalanced, and the children of these relationships will suffer the consequences. Many legal scholars are attempting to build a body of work that will allow for the expansion of traditional marriage. These results have been manifested in the "Beyond Conjugality" report in Canada and Al and Tipper Gore's Joined at the Heart *in the United States. Once the legal framework of marriage has changed, many will choose to marry simply for financial reasons, such as health insurance benefits. Marriage, as it has been known, will cease to exist.*

Marriage is a critical social institution. Stable families depend on it. Society depends on stable families. Up to now, with all the changes in marriage, the one thing we have been sure of is that marriage means monogamy. Gay marriage will break that connection. It will do this by itself, and by leading to polygamy and polyamory [multiple intimate relationships]. What lies beyond gay marriage is no marriage at all.

Stanley Kurtz, "Beyond 'Gay Marriage,'" *Catholic Insight*, February, 2004, pp. 12–14.

There is a rational basis for blocking both gay marriage and polygamy, and it does not depend upon a vague or religiously based disapproval of homosexuality or polygamy. Children need the stable family environment provided by marriage. In our individualist Western society, marriage must be companionate—and therefore monogamous. Monogamy will be undermined by gay marriage itself, and by gay marriage's ushering in of polygamy and polyamory.

The media's reflexive labeling of doubts about gay marriage as homophobia has made it almost impossible to debate the social effects of this reform. Advocacy of legalized polygamy is growing. A network of grassroots organizations seeking legal recognition for group marriage already exists. The cause of legalized group marriage is championed by a powerful faction of family law specialists. Influential legal bodies in both the United States and Canada have presented radical programs of marital reform. Some of these quasi-governmental proposals go so far as to suggest the abolition of marriage. The media and public spokesmen, meanwhile, treat the issue as an unproblematic advance for civil rights.

To consider what comes after gay marriage is not to say that gay marriage itself poses no danger to the institution of marriage. Quite apart from the likelihood that it will usher in legalized polygamy and polyamory, gay marriage will almost certainly weaken the belief that monogamy lies at the heart of marriage. But to see why this is so, we will first need to reconnoitre the slippery slope.

Promoting Polygamy and Polyamory

There are now many organizations favoring group marriage. And their strategy—their existence—owes much to the movement for gay marriage.

Why is state-sanctioned polygamy a problem? The deep reason is that it erodes the ethos of monogamous marriage. In most non-Western cultures, marriage is not a union of freely choosing individuals, but an alliance of family groups. The emotional relationship between husband and wife is attenuated and subordinated to the economic and political interests of extended kin. But in our [Western] world of freely choosing individuals, extended families fall away, and love and companionship are the only surviving principles on which families can be built. From [thirteenth-century theologian] Thomas Aquinas through [judge] Richard Posner, almost every serious observer has granted the incompatibility between polygamy and Western companionate marriage.

Polyamory comprises a bewildering variety of sexual combinations. There are triads of one woman and two men; heterosexual group marriages; groups in which some or all members are bisexual; lesbian groups, and so forth.

State-sanctioned polyamory is now the cutting-edge issue among scholars of family law.

Polyamorists are enthusiastic proponents of same-sex marriage. Obviously, any attempt to restrict marriage to a single man and woman would prevent the legalization of polyamory. After passage of the [American] Defense of Marriage Act in 1996, an article appeared in *Loving More*, the flagship magazine of the polyamory movement, calling for the creation of a polyamorist rights movement modeled on the movement for gay rights. The piece was published under the pen name Joy Singer, identified as the graduate of a "top ten law school" and a political organizer and public official in California for the previous two decades.

Marriages based on modern principles of companionate love, without religious rules and restraints, are unstable. Like the short-lived hippie communes, group marriages will be broken on the contradiction between companionate love and group solidarity. And children will pay the price.

Family Law Radicals

State-sanctioned polyamory is now the cutting-edge issue among scholars of family law. The preeminent school of thought in academic family law has its origins in the arguments of radical gay activists who once opposed same-sex marriage.

"Being queer," said one of its leading advocates, Paula Ettelbrick, "means pushing the parameters of sex and family, and in the process transforming the very fabric of society."

Paula Ettelbrick, Nancy Polikoff, Martha Fineman, Martha Ertman, Judith Stacey, David Chambers, and Martha Minow are among the most prominent family law theorists in the country. They have plenty of followers and hold much of the power and initiative within their field. There may be other approaches to academic family law, but none exceed the radicals in influence.

Canada. The first real public triumph of the family law radicals came in Canada. In 1972, [Canadian Prime Minister Pierre] Trudeau established the Law Commission of Canada to serve Parliament and the Justice Ministry as a kind of advisory board on legal reform. It was dissolved by Prime Minister [Brian] Mulroney but immediately revived by Jean Chretien on his election as prime minister in 1993. In December 2001, the commission submitted a report to Parliament called "Beyond Conjugality", which stops just short of recommending the abolition of marriage in Canada.

"Beyond Conjugality" contains three basic recommendations. First, judges are directed to concentrate on whether the individuals before them are "functionally interdependent," regardless of their actual marital status. On that theory, a household consisting of an adult child still living with his mother might be treated as the functional equivalent of a married couple. In so disregarding marital status, the report is clearly drawing on the work of [Harvard Law School professor Martha] Minow. . . .

The report's second key recommendation is that a legal structure be established allowing people to register their personal relationships with the government. Not only could heterosexual couples register as official partners, so could gay couples, adult children living with parents, and siblings or friends sharing a house. Although the authors are politic enough to relegate the point to footnotes, they state that they see no reason, in principle, to limit registered partnerships to two people.

The final recommendation of "Beyond Conjugality"—legalization of same-sex marriage—drew the most publicity when the report was released. Yet for the Law Commission of Canada, same-sex marriage is clearly just one part of the larger project of doing away with marriage itself. "Beyond Conjugality" stops short of recommending the abolition of legal marriage. The authors glumly note that, for the moment, the public is unlikely to accept such a step.

The text of "Beyond Conjugality", its bibliography, and the Law Commission of Canada's other publications unmistakably reveal the influence of the radical theorists who now dominate the discipline of family law. Collapsing the distinction between cohabitation and marriage is a proposal especially damaging to children, who are decidedly better off when born to married parents.

Joined at the Heart. Further confirmation, if any were needed, of the mainstream influence of the family law radicals came with Al and Tipper Gore's 2002 book (Al was the U.S. vice president under [Bill] Clinton) *Joined at the Heart*, in which they define a family as those who are "joined at the heart" (rather than by blood or by law). The notion that a family is any group "joined at the heart" comes straight from Martha Minow, who worked with the Gores. In fact, the article from which the Gores take their definition of family is also the one in which Minow tentatively floats the idea of substituting domestic partnership registries for traditional marriage.... So one of the guiding spirits of Canada's "Beyond Conjugality" report almost had a friend in the White House.

The trouble is, gay marriage itself threatens the ethos of monogamy.

Gay Marriages of Convenience

Polygamy, polyamory, and the abolition of marriage are bad ideas. But what has that got to do with gay marriage? The reason these ideas are connected is that gay marriage is increasingly being treated as a civil rights issue. Once we concede this, it becomes next to impossible to deny that same right to polygamists, polyamorists, or even cohabiting relatives and friends. And once everyone's relationship is recognized, marriage is gone, and only a system of flexible relationship contracts is left. The only way to stop gay marriage from launching a slide down this slope is if there is a compelling state interest in blocking polygamy or polyamory that does not also apply to gay marriage. Many would agree that the state has an interest in preventing polygamy and polyamory from undermining the ethos of monogamy at the core of marriage. The trouble is, gay marriage itself threatens the ethos of monogamy.

The "conservative" case for gay marriage holds that state-sanctioned marriage will reduce gay male promiscuity. But what if the effect works in reverse? What if, instead of marriage reducing gay promiscuity, sexually open gay couples help redefine marriage as a non-monogamous institution? There is evidence that this is exactly what will happen.

Even moderate gay advocates of same-sex marriage grant that, at present, gay male relationships are far less monogamous than heterosexual relationships. And there is a persuasive literature on this subject: Gabriel Rotello's *Sexual Ecology*, for example, offers a documented and powerful account of the behavioral and ideological barriers to monogamy among gay men.

Ironically, the form of gay matrimony that may pose the greatest threat to the institution of marriage involves heterosexuals. A Brigham Young University professor, Alan J. Hawkins, suggests an all-too-likely scenario in which two heterosexuals of the same sex might marry as a way of obtaining financial benefits. Consider the plight of an underemployed and uninsured single mother in her early thirties who sees little real prospect of marriage (to a man) in her future. Suppose she has a good friend, also female and heterosexual, who is single and childless but employed with good spousal benefits. Sooner or later, friends like this are going to start contracting same-sex marriages of convenience. The single mom will get medical and governmental benefits, will share her friend's paycheck, and will gain an additional caretaker for the kids besides. Her friend will gain companionship and a family life. The marriage would obviously be sexually open. And if lightning struck and the right man came along for one of the women, they could always divorce and marry heterosexually.

8

Same-Sex Marriage Will Not Lead to Legalized Polygamy

Kira Cochrane

Kira Cochrane is the women's editor for the Guardian *and writes a regular column in the* New Statesman.

Thanks to the popularity of HBO's Big Love, *a program offering a positive portrayal of polygamy, group marriage has become a popular topic. Critics, however, have begun to argue that if gay marriage is legalized, mayhem will follow, starting with legalized polygamy and eventually leading to the legalization of bizarre and formally taboo sexual practices. Gay marriage, however, has little in common with polygamy. Multiple marriages complicate an institution that is already complicated enough, while gay marriage—with two adults agreeing to a committed relationship—is basically conservative. The idea that the legalization of gay marriage will lead to polygamy is simply false.*

Blame it on Tom Hanks. (No, not for *Forrest Gump*. Come on, guys, that was years ago.) No, this time Hanks is in the frame to become an executive producer of the drama series *Big Love*, which has been running in the United States for a month or so, and causing quite a rumpus. About a polygamist family in Utah (one husband, three wives), this broadly sympathetic show has put group marriage under the spotlight at a time when a wave of polygamist activism is sweeping the nation, including a federal lawsuit that is challenging antipolygamy legislation.

These events have left conservative commentators asplutter about how the, so far unsuccessful, campaign for gay marriage in the United States is opening the floodgates for all sorts of relationships to be considered under the law. This "slippery slope" argument was first made by Senator Rick Santorum in 2003. "If the Supreme Court says that you have the right to consensual [gay] sex within your home," he said, "then you have the right to bigamy, you have the right to polygamy, you have the right to incest. . . ."

This conflation of gay marriage with polygamy and incest naturally pisses off America's gay-rights activists. Conservative commentators justify their position by stating that marriage has historically involved two fundamental components: first, two people; second, two people of opposite sexes. Remove either of these, they suggest, and the entire structure collapses. It's a view that many in Britain take as well. Writing in her blog, the British columnist Melanie Phillips has said: "As some of us predicted, the next sexual frontier to be conquered after gay marriage is . . . polygamy . . . So now anything goes—and our society is steadily going, as a result. Polyandry, polyamory, polygamy, polymorphism—can paedophilia, necrophilia, and bestiality be far behind?"

All of which makes for a very convenient and portentous argument against gay marriage, perfectly tuned to scare the horses and all other mammals besides. (A future in which a man might marry his sister, his mother and his Labrador! Yikes!) Realistically, though, it seems like baloney.

Liberal polygamy is just too variable.

The Gay Marriage and Polygamy Divide

For the fact is that gay marriage, a marriage between two consenting and unrelated adults, is analogous with straight marriage in a way that polygamy (and all the other suggested options) can never be. The United Kingdom has taken this on board with the recent implementation of civil partnerships for gay couples. If, socially and legally, marriage is primarily an engine for cohesion, designed to create stable and healthy family units from which both partners are discouraged to stray, then clearly, it seems in society's best interests to allow gay marriage. On a personal level, too, with most people recognizing that a gay identity is innate, it would be highly discriminatory not to.

When it comes to questions of discrimination, some polyamorists (people who openly have more than one lover, but are not married) are arguing that their need for more than one partner is as innate and discrete as a "gay" disposition, and should be recognized as such. But let's face it—this is going to take some proving. Most people in a long-term relationship have felt a strong need for another partner—a sudden, blinding attraction for a girl in a bar or a guy at the office—whether they pursue it or not. The sheer prevalence of this "disposition", this yearning for more sexual partners, would seem more a justification for abandoning marriage altogether than a case for extending its constructs.

Don't get me wrong: if people want to live communally, forming a long string of relationships, picking up new partners and discarding old ones, or remaining for many years in a stable collective of three or four or 27 people, that's entirely their call.

The conservative/religious model of polygamy is a feudal system in which the husband is overlord.

Conservative and Liberal Polygamy

It would make no sense, however, to write this into law. Liberal polygamy is just too variable. What happens if one partner in a group of three decides to leave, for instance? Are the remaining two still married? And what if two of the three partners are happy with the setup, but the other wants to invite more people into the marriage? Marriage is potentially rocky enough when there are two people involved, but the endless permutations of polygamy are impossible.

This probably explains why polygamy has usually taken a much more conservative form: what might be called the "harem" model (as seen in *Big Love*). The Web site for the U.S. Christian polygamy organization TruthBearer.org makes it very clear that "This is NOT about polyandry": God forbid that a woman should take more than one husband. Instead, the conservative/religious model of polygamy is a feudal system in which the husband is overlord. Rather than being in any way progressive, this setup takes us back to a time when all notions of equality were moot.

Given the inherent differences, it is to be hoped that this conflation of gay marriage with polygamy will end in the United States. To claim that there is an overlap or a "slippery slope" is entirely specious. The polyamorists will likely continue, separately, to try to convince us of their cause, and they are welcome to give it a go.

If they should ever succeed, after all, it could be one helluva wedding party.

9

Polygamy Violates Women's Rights

Lyn Cockburn

Lyn Cockburn writes for the Edmonton Sun *and* Herizons.

Polygamy is a harmful religious practice that exploits women. In the polygamous community of Bountiful, British Columbia, young girls are forced to marry older men. Unfortunately, the Canadian government has been reluctant to prosecute the community on the grounds of religious freedom. Complete religious freedom, however, would allow for many unjust practices. Some critics have argued that the legalization of gay marriage will lead to the legalization of polygamy. This argument, however, ignores the difference between gay consenting adults and young women forced into marriage. The Canadian government should shut down the Bountiful community.

In an effort to maintain a facade of sanity, I try to look upon most things in life through a prism of humor.

Sometimes this works well, as with Mahmoud Ahmadinejad, the so-called president of Iran. He's the dude who insists Israel should be moved to Europe and that the Holocaust is a hoax. The joke is, of course, on him, because he only thinks he's the president of Iran. There is no Iran.

On the other hand, polygamy ain't funny. This so-called religious practice demeans and degrades girls and women—to the point where girls in their early teens are forced to marry

50-year-old men. Where education is minimal. Where young girls who ought to be laughing, dancing, and playing ball are pregnant—for the second time.

Although, to keep from exploding in anger, I do try to think of all polygamist men as fat little creatures 4'9" in height with hairy long arms. . . .

Particularly unfunny is the polygamous community of Bountiful in eastern British Columbia, which provincial governments of various political stripes have managed to ignore for over 60 years.

Note that Winston Blackmore, the former bishop of Bountiful, had 28 wives in 2001 and 80 children, numbers which have probably since increased.

Every time someone suggests the place ought to be shut down once and for all, some governmental idiot mumbles that the Bountiful lawyers might mount a Supreme Court challenge and win—on the grounds of religious freedom.

Every religion follows some practices that are best put in the garbage can.

The Canadian Government and Religious Freedom

Now that is mildly amusing. If Canadians permitted every person of religious faith in Canada to carry out every practice of his religion, we'd have a most peculiar—and unjust—society. Every religion follows some practices that are best put in the garbage can. In other words, it is not just Christianity which produces wackos—who, for example, would deny condoms to countries with the highest incidence of AIDS and would like to teach "intelligent design" in science classes.

Speaking of schools, the ones in Bountiful teach the righteousness and joys of polygamy—surely an example of brainwashing. These schools are government funded. Few girls complete high school. That is not funny.

Even harder to laugh at is the recent study commissioned by the feds that recommends decriminalizing polygamy—because a Charter challenge might be successful and because polygamy has rarely been prosecuted in Canada. The punch line to that insane joke ought to be, of course: Let's shut down Bountiful and any other community like it and ensure that Canadian women are not degraded in this manner.

Making it almost impossible to smile are those pundits who posit the "What did you expect when you legalized same-sex marriage?" argument. These laughable people insist that altering the traditional view of marriage in any way opens the door for unknown perversions: polygamy; polyamorous marriage—this is evidently the union of groups of men and women; and, no doubt, the marriage of a man and his best friend, the family sheepdog.

Let us not forget the reality of young girls forced into marriage with men old enough to be their grandfathers.

All of which ignores the fact that polygamy exploits girls and women. Let us not forget the reality of young girls forced into marriage with men old enough to be their grandfathers. Gay marriage, of course, is a union entered into by two consenting adults. Many of these couples have been together longer than many straight couples

As I said, polygamy ain't funny. Although some of the people who support, condone, or excuse it are.

Maybe "peculiar" is a better word for them. Insensitive? Misguided? Stupid, inhumane. . . . I'm getting angry again.

All male polygamists are 4'9" with long hairy arms. . . . All male polygamists are. . . .

I don't feel better. I am not laughing. And I won't 'til the Canadian government shuts down Bountiful and ensures that such exploitative communities may never again exist in Canada.

10

Polygamy Does Not Violate Women's Rights

Maggi

Maggi belongs to a Mississippi group that practices polygamy.

According to Maggi, the life of a sisterwife—one of several wives who share one husband—may not be a perfect life, but it is nonetheless a satisfying life. In Maggi's family, each wife takes turns sleeping in the same bed with the husband, while the first wife is responsible for settling any disputes between wives. Some wives work, while others stay at home, and the multiple incomes cover the regular bills plus provide each sisterwife an equal allowance. One of the biggest disadvantages of sharing a husband is that sex is infrequent; this is complicated if the husband is important within the church, a position that requires him to marry more wives than other members. Wives, however, have no power to make decisions regarding new wives.

We all live in the same house. We have a bunk bed, double on the bottom and single on the top. Husband, first wife, and the "ON" wife sleep on the bottom and the other two "OFF" wives sleep above. We find this very intimate as we all are sleeping in the same bed though on different levels, and we can still feel and hear what is happening when sex happens in our bed.

Relationships between us sisterwives are mainly quite good, as our first wife Hanna is the main force in our household

Maggi, "The Life of a 'Sisterwife,'" The *Guardian*, November 21, 2006. Reproduced by permission of Guardian News Service, Ltd. Available at www.guardian.co.uk/religion/ Story/0,,1953263,00.html.

and will settle most of the disputes between the other wives herself without our husband being involved. There are jealousies—this is inevitable between any group of women living closely together. Our husband does his best to be fair to all of us, but we all have our own opinion of what is fair, don't we.

Sex, now that is the big one. In our household we have one week (but only on six days we can have sex with him) sleeping with our husband and three weeks off. Our first wife has the Saturdays with our husband in addition to her week so she gets four extra days with him in each cycle. That's why she sleeps on the lower bunk every night with the "ON" wife. In reality we have sex in an average week about two to three times in the six days we can have sex with our husband. Though it's not totally satisfying (two or three times a month) for us we do find that having a week with our husband is the better method then the one-night method used by others.

Income, Allowances, and Sex

Money, well we have four incomes in our household. Our husband, Brian, is an accountant, first wife Hanna is the deputy headteacher at the local elementary school, second wife Mary is a nurse, I'm the stay-at-home wife (I look after the children under school age and do the cleaning, washing, and generally look after the house), that's my job, fourth wife Mary-Jane, she is a teacher at the same elementary school as Hanna. On Sunday and when the other wives come home, they do the ironing, some of the cooking, and the gardening.

All income from the wives goes into the same account and each wife gets the same allowance for her personal needs, the rest is saved for special events and needs for us wives. Husband's income pays for all the household bills as would be normal in any marriage, and he has his allowance that comes from his account.

No, we don't have physical relationships between sister-wives because it's not permitted in our religion. We sleep with our arms on top of our bed covers so it doesn't happen. And in any case if any wife was foolish enough to try, all would feel it in our bed; a simple rule—no touching or kissing in bed or at any other time between one woman and another sisterwife and another.

I love being in a polygamous family and my sisterwives agree with me.

As for sex, no we don't get very much actual sex (i.e., our husband entering us), but he does work very hard and sometimes quite late so a wife cannot expect him to perform every night.

I love being in a polygamous family and my sisterwives agree with me. The downside is the sex. Not the quality, I have no complaints about that, but just the quantity, and we all know that it will get worse when the final two wives join in the next two to three years. Then it will be like two to three times in six weeks. As you go higher in the temple government, the more wives you have to have, and as our husband has been appointed as group treasurer and deputy convenor of our temple, it means he now must have six wives. Us wives get no say in how many wives our husband has, but we do have a big say in who joins us—as a sisterwife it's really the only power we have.

11

Polyandry Would Be Used Against Women

Kaimi

Kaimi covers Mormon issues in a number of publications.

While polygamy can mean men or women having more than one spouse in theory, most often the term polygamy is used synonymously with polygyny—one man taking multiple wives. Polyandry, one woman choosing multiple husbands, is seldom considered an option. In theory, polyandry could be viewed as a profeminist arrangement. In practice, however, the promotion of polyandry is problematic, because it traditionally has been used against women. Ideally, polyandry would create equality within Mormon communities; in reality, it would probably be antifeminist.

From a feminist perspective, is polyandry more or less acceptable than polygyny?

Let's start with a very quick history and terminology lesson. Polygamy means taking more than one spouse, either husband or wife. Polygyny means one man taking multiple wives. Polyandry means one woman taking multiple husbands.

On an initial examination, polyandry seems to have some potential to be a profeminist piece in the polygamy puzzle.

In the Mormon context, there are two twists to these definitions. First, the term polygamy is often used informally, to

Kaimi, "Polyandry," *Feminist Mormon Housewives.org*, August 14, 2006. Reproduced by permission. Available at www.feministmormonhousewives.org/?p=697.

mean polygyny. Second, the term polyandry is typically used to refer to the practice of male-initiated marriage and sexual relations with already-married women. As a definitional matter, "polyandry" need not be limited to male-initiated bonds, and in some polyandrous societies, women have freedom to choose their mates. However, Mormon polyandry as practiced in Nauvoo [Illinois] (and later to a lesser degree in Utah) did not accord women such freedom. Rather, a small subset of already-married women were approached and asked to become the plural wives of other men, while simultaneously remaining in their existing marriages. . . .

Polyandry thus forces men to internalize some of the costs of polygamy, rather than offloading all of the costs onto women.

Polyandry Creates New Problems

On an initial examination, polyandry seems to have some potential to be a profeminist piece in the polygamy puzzle. For one thing, it adds a very satisfying "sauce for the goose, sauce for the gander" aspect to the discussion. The system of Mormon polygyny institutionalized yet another gender-based double standard. This double standard placed the brunt of the emotional costs on the plural wives, who were expected to share their husbands. Under polyandry, the costs of spouse-sharing are distributed at least somewhat among both sexes.

Second, polyandry probably fosters male empathy toward women forced to share spouses. Polygamous marriages often created tension and unhappiness in women, who dealt with difficult emotional turmoil. Similarly, we read of tension and unhappiness felt by men who were in polyandrous marriages. [Mormon] Henry Jacobs wrote that "I feel alone and no one to speak to call my own. I feel like a lamb without a mother." . . .

As painful as these passages are, they are striking because they are male-authored; normally such bleak narratives come from women in polygamous marrriages. Absent the threat of polyandry, it is easy for men to sit around and blithely discuss the need for wives to share a husband—after all, men reap all of the benefits and feel none of the loss. It is quite another thing for men to be forced to internalize these questions. In a polyandrous society, the analysis for men moves away from "women should be happy to share their spouses" and becomes a self-query of "would I be happy to share my spouse?"

Polyandry thus forces men to internalize some of the costs of polygamy, rather than offloading all of the costs onto women.

Third, polyandry potentially allows more freedom for women to enter into fulfilling relationships. Mormon polyandry, as practiced, may not appear to grant this benefit. (This is because all polyandrous marriages were male-initiated, and mostly initiated by a small group of high-level church leaders.) However, it seems likely that even in a society where only male-initiated polyandry were allowed, women could use informal means to enter into relationships that they felt were desirable. That is, a woman could approach a desired suitor and suggest that he request her hand as a polyandrous bride. Thus, polyandry could become a potential avenue for women to seek and maintain fulfilling relationships with desired partners.

On all of these counts—lessening of the double standard, greater burden-sharing and probably empathy from men, and broader relationship opportunities for women—polyandry seems like a clear gain for women.

Polyandry Has Serious Drawbacks

First, in a system of Mormon polyandry, such as was practiced in Nauvoo and later to a lesser degree in Utah, polyandrous marriages were limited to male-initiated relationships. This placed certain limitations on the broader level of relationship choice for women. It is possible that women could informally circumvent these limits, as noted above. Nevertheless, a system of Mormon polyandry does not grant women the same degree of freedom as men to enter into relationships that they feel are desirable. It is the rule of male-initiated polyandry that imposes these limits, and so allowing for informal female-initiated polyandry helps ameliorate the problem, but does not do away with it entirely.

Second, it seems possible that polyandry would result in loss of status for participating women because of differing societal expecations and perceptions of male versus female sexual boundaries. Men who have sexual relations with multiple women are often viewed as powerful and desirable; women who have sexual relations with multiple men are often perceived as loose or trashy. It seems possible that polyandry would have serious negative social consequences.

Another concern is that forms of male-initiated polyandry seem similar to societal attitudes treating women as chattel [property or slaves]. Much of the Biblical polyandry—such as David and Michael—takes place as men blithely decide amongst themselves how the "property" is shared; women are left powerless, treated as mere prizes to be won. To the extent that male-initiated polyandry depends on or reinforces that dynamic, it is obviously not a net gain for women.

The most striking argument against Mormon polyandry, though, is found in its history. The history of Mormon polyandry has been starkly antifeminist—often seeming to boil down to old and problematic dynamic of multiple men competing for sexual access to attractive women. In that sense, male-initiated polyandry symbolizes all that is wrong with patriarchal power structures and oppression of women.

Polyandry Would Not Benefit Women

Records of polyandry as practiced suggest that it did not afford greater relationship choices to women, but rather created extra layers of angst and heartache within their existing relationships. The story of Zina Diantha Huntington Jacobs Smith Young is instructive. Zina twice entered into polyandrous marriages; at least one of them caused her quite a bit of anguish. She received a polyandrous marriage proposal from Joseph Smith while she was married to Henry Jacobs. She struggled with this idea, writing that it was a greater sacrifice than giving her life; ultimately she acquiesced only when Joseph told her that an angel would slay him if she did not marry him.

She writes less about her polyandrous marriage to Brigham Young, but notes that she felt "weakness of heart" after it. For Zina, polyandry did not create more opportunities for her to explore fruitful relationships—rather, it added stress and pain to the relationships that she had.

Polyandry would not be a more feminist version of polygamy; in practice, it would almost certainly be more antifeminist.

In theory, polyandry could be a version of polygamy that is more feminist-friendly than classic polygyny. As noted above, it removes some of the double standard, and it seems to create—again, in theory—additional opportunities for women to enter into rewarding relationships.

However, the history of polyandry as practiced, and the relationship limitations imposed under a system of male-initiated polyandry, weigh more heavily on the other side of the balance. Polyandry would not be a more feminist version of polygamy; in practice, it would almost certainly be more antifeminist. There aren't very many institutions that can make a culture of male-initiated polygyny look good by comparison—but a male-initiated system of polyandry is probably one of them.

12

Polygamy Honors Cultural Traditions

Nehanda Imara

Nehanda Imara is a pan-African activist, writer, and mother.

If there is a male shortage within the African American community, then polygamy may offer a workable option for women. Marriage remains an important institution within African American culture, but perhaps the institution—as it exists—can be overvalued. In a sense, adultery, which has been frequently accepted if not approved of, is "unofficial polygamy." Traditional African communities had a more open mind toward marriage, and some African American women have drawn on these traditions. By allowing men to marry multiple women, men are less likely to seek outside relationships. Legalizing polygamy may even allow men and women to build more lasting marriages.

Maybe it's just me, but as a divorced woman of African descent, I am more often contemplating the question: Is polygamy a possible solution to the male shortage in our community?

Have I limited my options by only considering brothers born in America? Is the male shortage real? Or perceived? When I find myself answering, "Yes," to all of the above, I feel fatigued by the prospects. What are my chances of meeting a brother who wants to deal with my independence, my passion as an activist? And even though I know I'm getting better with each passing year, I am over forty.

Nehanda Imara, "Reconsidering Polygamy," *I've Known Rivers: The MoAD Stories Project,* June, 2006. Reproduced by permission of the author.

Five hundred years removed from mother Africa, I would argue that polygamy is one of our African cultural retentions. In its various forms it is not necessarily preferred, but it is tolerated. Most of us can remember hearing our mother, auntie, or grandma speaking of so-and-so who had another family "on the side."

Growing up in America, I was taught that marriage is a highly revered social function within the African community. Without it, somehow, you are not complete, not fully adult. Once visiting Ghana I was once told that a grown woman is still considered to be a child until married with children.

Marriage, Adultery, and Polygamy

When I was in my twenties and met my ex-husband I was full of hope, idealism, and romance about our union. But these days I am more practical. I have the same basic desires as my sisters; I want a positive, healthy relationship—with a brother. I want to share a meaningful life with "my man" and have peace of mind. Of course I realize that the African community in America has historically been confronted with decades of systemic economic inequities and social injustices that challenge this desire. Yet, in spite of these obstacles and daily struggles, we as a community share a collective yearning for a "normal" life.

As a divorced, single woman, I often feel a personal rage for the subtle judgements I receive from family, society, and myself for not "holding onto my husband." Most people think marriage is as normal as getting a job or owning a house. Unmarried, you will not enjoy a full menu of life. The perception is that your life lacks the most important ingredients and spices.

Have I put too much weight on the value of marriage? No! I do want a partnership and companion for life. Yes. I want the respect, consideration, and status that comes with the title, "wife." But what about "cowife?"

There is nothing in my background that has prepared me to accept polygamy, so why would I consider it as a possible option today? I realize, like most women, regardless of our social, economic, and cultural status, we will at least once in our life share a male significant other with another woman. Sharing a male significant other with another woman is usually seen simultaneously as inevitable, but extremely undesirable. Sharing is also sometimes known as "cheating," "adultery," "relationship betrayal," or "unofficial polygamy." Each of these social improprieties seems to carry the weight of being an immoral person, but it is a sometimes tolerated act.

Do I, as an African woman accept "relationship betrayal" because it is inevitable? No. Are brothers naturally polygamous? Most will tell you they are.

The African extended family is the glue that has kept our community together this long.

The Resilient African Family

As an activist I have studied African culture (traveled and lived in Africa and the African Diaspora) and have concluded that the African family is resilient and multifaceted. The extended family is more than a notion. The African extended family is the glue that has kept our community together this long. The !Kung (also known as the "Bushmen of the Kalahari") believe sole commitment to one person is the ultimate human goal and 99 percent of their society achieve this. The !Kung also have a practice called, "trial marriage," where multiple divorces are allowed until a couple are mature enough. By the third or forth trial their "hearts have grown big" toward each other and they stay together forever. Polygamy is also tolerated by the !Kung, but not preferred.

I have some "sista-friends" currently in open "polygamous" relationships. I recently asked Maya (not her real name) how she developed her ideas about polygamy, and if it really worked for her. Maya grew up as a teenager around Black Panthers and black Muslims at a time when polygamy was more openly discussed. She grew to accept the idea. Her husband is a Muslim and has accepted this all of his life. I asked her if she would have felt differently if she had been the first wife instead of the second?

"No. Because it's illegal in this country, most people don't ever discuss it," she said. "Most married men have another woman anyway. A lot of women silently accept this. I do, too, but not silently. I just happen to know her. And we know our husband is not sleeping around getting diseases and stuff. Deep down most women just want their man to themselves. This would be the perfect thing. But, in our imperfect understanding of the world men tend to want more than one woman. Why, I don't know. It must be in their blood. I do know I'd like to have a man, than to be alone."

Polygamy as an Alternative

Relationships are like food; we need them to survive. Within each relationship our hearts seek love, on whatever terms, definitions, or flavors we have come to call it. Marriage becomes the main dish on this menu. Maya also said she thought that "most American men (black or white) are afraid to ask their wives to become polygamous because they think she'll leave." Maya believes that once a woman accepts her husband loving two women and she's not afraid that he'll leave, then she will become secure, even appreciate the new family setup.

Legalized polygamy just might lower the divorce rate.

Of course, Maya knows her situation is very specific. "This is easy for me to say as the second wife, because I want to share. But I have been blessed with a husband and cowife who grew up accepting this as natural. I like the fact that he has a week with me, and then I have time to myself. I was single for a long time, so this is like having my cake and eating it too."

I am still not convinved about polygamy as a natural alternative. It works for my friend but certainly won't work for most of today's black women in America. Still, it is a centuries-long tradition that may still hold some benefits in today's society. So why not legalize it? Legalized polygamy just might lower the divorce rate. What do you think?

13

Serial Marriage and Promiscuity Are No Different Than Polygamy

George Neumayr

George Neumayr is editor of Catholic World Report *and a columnist for* California Political Review.

While critics have seen HBO's new series Big Love *as progressive in treating the subject of polygamy, in reality, the program simply reflects contemporary lifestyles. While polygamy may be illegal, men and women no longer believe in lasting, committed sexual relationships. Polygamy, like the concept of gay unions, borrows from pre-Christian philosophy: human nature, in matters of sexuality, cannot be helped. Promiscuity and serial marriages, finally, are no different than polygamous ones.*

Actor Bill Paxton has told the press that one of the sources of inspiration for his character on HBO's drama about polygamy, *Big Love*, is Bill Clinton. That's a telling comment. It suggests the reason why the show generates a ho-hum reaction: a Clintonian culture of promiscuity, adultery, and open marriage is already polygamous in its logic, even if it hasn't gotten around to enshrining polygamy in law.

A culture of routine divorce also makes polygamy thinkable. After all, like Paxton's character, many Americans have had three spouses. Just not simultaneously. Isn't the show's concept of a harried man juggling multiple wives just a small

George Neumayr, "HBO's 'Big Love': What Taboo?" *Human Events*, March 20, 2006. Reproduced by permission. Available at www.humanevents.com/article.php?id=13352.

extension of the divorce comedy genre? The creators of the show have talked about overcoming the "yuck factor." But that shouldn't be too hard, given that characters carrying on with many women at once is a staple of most shows.

The simultaneous sexual carrying on of polygamy is somewhat more obvious and centralized than other forms of promiscuity, but it is essentially indistinguishable from the alternative lifestyles based upon promiscuity the culture has already absorbed. If Paxton sees Bill Clinton as a model for polygamists, that's because promiscuity/open marriage and polygamy aren't very far apart, differing not in their essence but in their outward appearance.

In a culture of habitual divorce and promiscuity, Americans, whether they realize it or not, accept the core claim of polygamy.

A Culture of Divorce and Promiscuity

The show can't topple any taboos in this area because there are none left. In a culture of habitual divorce and promiscuity, Americans, whether they realize it or not, accept the core claim of polygamy: that sexual love needn't be exclusive, permanent, and undivided.

Here again, Hollywood isn't so much driving the culture as cementing it, taking attitudes widely in circulation and implicit in approved practices and improvising them. It ups the ante a little bit by portraying them in rare and superficially stigmatized (but not morally condemned in any real way) settings. Hollywood's challenge is not so much to overcome the yuck factor as the yawn factor.

Press accounts about *Big Love* have noted that its creators are gay, which underscores that the opposition to polygamy from gay activists over the last few years is nothing more than political posturing. They know that polygamy is perfectly consistent with the logic underlying same-sex marriage but can't say that lest it stall that drive.

Once marriage is accepted as "man-made," humans can make it, unmake it, and remake it at will. And after that point any prohibitions are simple arbitrariness. Gay activists, for largely public relations reasons, will sometimes insist upon the sacredness of "two," which is oddly arbitrary, since they justify their position on the grounds that marriage has no natural, preexisting character to it. At least the creators of *Big Love* are ignoring this fakery and following the premises of same-sex marriage to its logical conclusion.

Polygamy and Pre-Christian Values

It is revealing that press stories about the show barely even mention the impact of the polygamous arrangement on the children in it. The impression left is that if polygamy is morally problematic at all that's only because it is unfair to the wives. But that problem disappears through modern life's favorite absolutions—"choice" and "consent."

To the extent that children are even factored into the moral equation, polygamists are now borrowing another handy fallacy from the gay-marriage movement: the principle that children need one father and one mother permanently interested in them is mere prejudice and not a reflection of the natural law. Say polygamists: If Heather has three mothers instead of two, so what? Doesn't society now say that families are self-defined and that love, in whatever package it comes, is more important than adhering to natural form?

The wall protecting marriage as exclusive and permanent was long ago breached.

Polygamy is a guaranteed beneficiary of avant-garde moral philosophy, because for all of its claims of progress it is basically a return to the practices of antiquity and pre-Christian paganism. It is ironic that at least on this front the modern West and world of Islam overlap. They are both in their own ways old ideologies of intemperance catered to fallen human nature, and they are both polygamous in their ethos.

The West promises multiple partners in this life; Islam promises many in the next. Where the West offers a menu of promiscuity, certain branches of Islam offer "temporary wives." Men in the West can discard their wives through easy no-fault divorce; some sects of Islam permit men to divorce their wives by simply saying, "I divorce you."

Western secularism and Islam share an antipathy for the hard sayings of Christianity, one of which revolves around the indissolubility of marriage. There is no reason why a de-Christianized culture in the West won't gradually become as polygamous as those in the East. The wall protecting marriage as exclusive and permanent was long ago breached.

14

Polygamy Is a Deterrent to Democracy

Tom Flanagan

Tom Flanagan is professor of political science at the University of Calgary.

Most people do not realize that the legalization of polygamy will have a broad impact on democracy. Although polygamous nations like China and Japan developed great civilizations in the past, they never developed ideas of equality before the law and individual rights. Because wealthier males will marry more than one wife in a polygamous society, less prosperous males become alienated from the culture, sometimes leading to criminal behavior. This forces polygamous societies to enforce harsh penalties to maintain social order. War is also a frequent reality for polygamous cultures, as men search for new women beyond their national borders.

Polygamists at Bountiful, British Columbia, have once again put multiple marriage up for debate in Canada. Most feminists want to keep the Criminal Code's prohibition, because polygamy puts women under patriarchal domination and leads to young girls being treated as chattel [property or slaves]. That's true, but we should also be concerned about the broader impact of polygamy on liberal democracy.

Constitutional government first arose in the monogamous societies of republican Greece and Rome and was later reborn in seventeenth-century Europe, where Christianity had

Tom Flanagan, "Our Sexual Constitution: The Link Between Monogamy and Democracy," *Globe and Mail*, September 9, 2007. Reproduced by permission of the author.

strengthened monogamy as a legal and social norm. The other great civilizations of China, Japan, India, the Middle East, and pre-Columbian America all tolerated or promoted polygamy. They can claim many brilliant achievements, but they never gave rise to equality before the law, individual rights, and self-government.

The first thing students learn in statistics courses is that "correlation is not causation." There has to be a deeper link between two phenomena before we can say that one is necessary to the other. What, then, is the connection between monogamy and democracy?

The Monogamy–Democracy Connection

The answer comes from evolutionary biology, which stresses the reproductive asymmetry of males and females, especially in mammalian species. Multiplication of sexual contacts will not multiply the number of offspring for females; but males, by multiplying their sexual encounters, can reap enormous payoffs in the Darwinian game of differential reproduction. How many children did Solomon have, with his 700 wives and 300 concubines?

Polygamous societies tend toward extreme authoritarianism and arbitrary government, with Draconian punishments to protect harems and control slaves and soldiers.

This is why polygamy (multiple marriage) almost always takes the form of polygyny (a husband with several wives) rather than polyandry (a wife with several husbands). The reproductive payoff to the female is always the same, but the payoff to the male can be enormously larger under polygyny than under polyandry or monogamy. Hence the universally observed tendency of males to pursue sexual opportunities more widely and aggressively than females do.

Natural selection has shaped us to learn some things more readily than others. People easily adopt polygyny, as both a social and a legal norm. In one large, often-cited study of more than 1,200 societies, 15 percent were monogamous, almost 85 percent were polygynous to some degree, and fewer than 1 percent were polyandrous.

When polygyny is practiced on a large scale, it polarizes the male population. On one side are the wealthy and powerful men of the ruling class, with their wives and concubines; on the other side are large numbers of poor and powerless men, deprived of the chance for marriage. Desperate for reproductive opportunities, surplus men are likely to become criminals, or to end up as soldiers or slaves, or even soldier-slaves, as were the Mamelukes and Janissaries of the Muslim empires.

The Polygamy–Authoritarian Connection

Polygamous societies tend toward extreme authoritarianism and arbitrary government, with Draconian punishments to protect harems and control slaves and soldiers. Driven by millenniums of evolutionary pressure, young men will take extreme chances to find sexual gratification, so there have to be extreme punishments to control their libidinous passions. There is also a tendency toward permanent warfare, because plundering neighboring peoples is the only way of satisfying the polygamous social system's limitless craving for women, slaves, and soldiers.

Simply put, polygamy raises reproductive stakes to levels that make it difficult for males to practice the self-restraint required by constitutional democracy.

Polygamous, authoritarian systems may achieve imperial conquest and cultural efflorescence, but they do not favor the growth of democracy. Based on arbitrary power, radical inequality, harsh laws and endless warfare, the milieu is the very opposite of constitutional democracy, which must rest on the rule of law, equality before the law, mild punishments, and peaceable exchange in free markets. Simply put, polygamy raises reproductive stakes to levels that make it difficult for males to practice the self-restraint required by constitutional democracy.

Of course, as long as social norms remain monogamous, Canada's democracy will not fail if a few fundamentalist Mormons in British Columbia, or polygamous African immigrants in Toronto, are not prosecuted for violating the Criminal Code. But that does not mean the law is unimportant, because legal norms tell us what social norms ought to be.

The legal equality of liberal democracy, which in the twentieth century gave us equal rights for men and women, is based on the social norm of monogamy, which provides rough equality of opportunity for men in the all-important game of reproduction. Regardless of what the British Columbia attorney general finally decides to do about the Bountiful polygamists, it's an occasion for reflecting on the sexual constitution underpinning our political constitution.

15

Polygamy Is No Deterrent to Democracy

Jack Cunningham

Jack Cunningham is a writer, editor, public opinion analyst, and political strategist.

The idea that the practice of polygamy will endanger democracy is a conclusion reached from faulty logic. Polygamy neither leads to incessant warfare nor criminal behavior. While nondemocratic societies may practice polygamy, polygamy does not create nondemocratic societies. Instead, many authoritarian societies practice polygamy simply because those in authority wish to, and are financially able to, have more than one wife. And while some authoritarian societies were known as warrior cultures, military practices were never built around controlling the male libido. Authoritarian power should be resisted, but blaming peripheral practices such as polygamy will prove to be a poor prevention strategy.

Thomas Flanagan, a University of Calgary political scientist and occasional adviser to Conservative politicians, who has written sensibly enough about other topics, graced the pages of last Tuesday's *Globe and Mail* with a rather eccentric op-ed. piece about polygamy. Not, to be sure, a matter anywhere near the top of any public agenda right now, but the existence of a few polygamists among the fundamentalist Mormon population of Bountiful, British Columbia, has led to

Jack Cunningham, "Prof. Flanagan on Polygamy," *Whig*, September 7, 2007. Reproduced by permission of the author. Available at http://whigca.blogspot.com/2007/09/prof-flanagan-on-polygamy.html.

speculation about their possible prosecution and started a modest debate that has the good professor somewhat perturbed. To Flanagan, polygamy (particularly polygyny, in which husbands take plural wives) is not merely bizarre or offensive, but a threat to democracy. "The legal equality of liberal democracy, which in the twentieth century gave us equal rights for men and women", he writes, "is based on the social norm of monogamy, which provides rough equality of opportunity for men in the all-important game of reproduction."

The notion that social conservatives like Flanagan are driven primarily by anxiety over sex is an old and largely discredited one.

The notion that social conservatives like Flanagan are driven primarily by anxiety over sex is an old and largely discredited one. But reasoning like this bids fair to revive it. Flanagan notes that early conceptions of constitutional government arose in the monogamous polities of ancient Greece and Rome, and later flourished in Christian Europe. Polygamy was more acceptable in other civilizations, which, whatever their merits, did not produce proto-democratic political ideas. Flanagan does concede the logical fallacy in inferring a causal link between two phenomena from the fact that they are often found together, but his subsequent argument for a link between monogamy and democracy shows he is no exemplar of restraint in such matters.

Widespread polygyny, he contends, "polarizes the male population" with "the wealthy and powerful men of the ruling class, with their wives and concubines" on one side, and on the other "large numbers of poor and powerless men, deprived of the chance for marriage." Thwarted in their quest to reproduce, these "surplus men are likely to become criminals, or to end up as soldiers or slaves, or even soldier-slaves, as were the Mamelukes and Janissaries of the Muslim empires."

Polygamous societies, he adds, "tend toward extreme authoritarianism and arbitrary government, with Draconian punishments to protect harems and control slaves and soldiers." The legions of sexually frustrated men will break the law to find gratification, "so there have to be extreme punishments to control their libidinous passions. There is also a tendency toward permanent warfare, because plundering neighboring peoples is the only way of satisfying the polygamous social system's limitless craving for women, slaves, and soldiers."

Polygamy Does Not Cause Authoritarianism

Yet polygamous arrangements tend to be peripheral features of the authoritarian regimes Flanagan describes, not their *raison d'etre*. The soldier-slave armies of the Muslim world were not a device for making use of men who could not find women, but a tool for extending the power of the ruler, and their existence was made possibly by slavery and the fact that prisoners of war had no alternative to joining them save death, not an overabundance of men who were luckless in seeking sexual release. The Janissaries of the Ottoman Empire were kept in barracks not so they would refrain from committing rape at every opportunity but to enforce iron discipline and group solidarity. In addition, they were allowed to marry after retirement, when their military utility was over and from the eighteenth century on, they were allowed to marry before that, provided their sons went into service. "Controlling their libidinous passions" was not an end in itself.

It is less that polygamy conduces to authoritarianism than that authoritarianism conduces to polygamy, by empowering the ruling caste to take what they want, in women as in other measures of status.

And, of course, polygyny was feasible only because the Sultan and his wealthy hangers-on enjoyed extraordinary legal and social privileges, and women could be treated as chattels. It is less that polygamy conduces to authoritarianism than that authoritarianism conduces to polygamy, by empowering the ruling caste to take what they want, in women as in other measures of status. The quasi-mythical institution of the *droit de seigneur*, in which the medieval lord would share the wedding bed of every virgin bride taken by those beneath him as a token of their dependence upon him, can be seen in the same light. The way to fight authoritarianism is to prevent the emergence of its central features, such as gross legal inequalities and arbitrary, concentrated power, not such efflorescences as harems.

As for inequalities in the pursuit of reproductive opportunity, all men have some nodding and bitter acquaintance with them, and know better than to expect them to fade. In his "What is to be Done", Lenin notoriously defined politics as "who does what to whom." Surely we need not join Professor Flanagan in adopting that definition so literal-mindedly.

16

Legal Polygamy Would Have Social Consequences

Jonathan Rauch

Jonathan Rauch is a senior writer and columnist for National Journal *and a frequent contributor to* Reason.

While libertarians habitually defend individual rights, the practice of polygamy will have a significant impact on society at large. Most often polygamy really means polygyny, the practice of one man marrying more than one woman. If legalized, polygynous relationships would allow wealthier men to marry more than one wife, eventually creating a male surplus. This would fall most heavily on poor, uneducated citizens, who would be unable to marry and have families. Many males, as history has shown, will turn to criminal behavior. Once the ratio of unmarried males grows wider (120 eligible males for every 100 eligible females), society itself becomes unstable. It has become common, even in small polygamous communities within the United States, to orphan young men so that older men within the communities can continue to have access to younger women. Polygamy may disguise itself as freedom of religion, but its potential for social harm should cause citizens to think carefully before making it legal.

"And now, polygamy," sighs Charles Krauthammer, in a recent *Washington Post* column. It's true. As if they didn't already have enough on their minds, Americans are going to have to debate polygamy. And not a moment too soon.

Jonathan Rauch, "One Man, Many Wives, Big Problems: The Social Consequences of Polygamy Are Bigger Than You Think," *Reason Magazine*, April 3, 2006. Reproduced by permission.

For generations, taboo kept polygamy out of sight and out of mind in America. But the taboo is crumbling. An HBO television series called *Big Love*, which benignly portrays a one-husband, three-wife family in Utah, set off the latest round of polygamy talk. Even so, a federal lawsuit (now on appeal), the American Civil Liberties Union's stand for polygamy rights, and the rising voices of pro-polygamy groups such as TruthBearer.org (an evangelical Christian group) and Principle Voices (which *Newsweek* describes as "a Utah-based group run by wives from polygamous marriages") were already making the subject hard to duck.

So far, libertarians and lifestyle liberals approach polygamy as an individual-choice issue, while cultural conservatives use it as a bloody shirt to wave in the gay-marriage debate. The broad public opposes polygamy but is unsure why. What hardly anyone is doing is thinking about polygamy as social policy.

If the coming debate changes that, it will have done everyone a favor. For reasons that have everything to do with its own social dynamics and nothing to do with gay marriage, polygamy is a profoundly hazardous policy.

The real-world practice of polygamy seems to flow from men's desire to marry all the women they can have children with.

Polygamy Really Means Polygyny

To understand why, begin with two crucial words. The first is "marriage." Group love (sometimes called polyamory) is already legal, and some people freely practice it. Polygamy asserts not a right to love several others but a right to marry them all. Because a marriage license is a state grant, polygamy is a matter of public policy, not just of personal preference.

The second crucial word is "polygyny." Unlike gay marriage, polygamy has been a common form of marriage since at least biblical times, and probably long before. In his 1994 book *The Moral Animal: The New Science of Evolutionary Psychology*, Robert Wright notes that a "huge majority" of the human societies for which anthropologists have data have been polygamous. Virtually all of those have been polygynous: that is, one husband, multiple wives. Polyandry (one wife, many husbands) is vanishingly rare. The real-world practice of polygamy seems to flow from men's desire to marry all the women they can have children with.

Moreover, in America today the main constituents for polygamous marriage are Mormons and, as *Newsweek* reports, "a growing number of evangelical Christian and Muslim polygamists." These religious groups practice polygyny, not polyandry. Thus, in light of current American politics as well as copious anthropological experience, any responsible planner must assume that if polygamy were legalized, polygynous marriages would outnumber polyandrous ones—probably vastly.

Here is something else to consider: As far as I've been able to determine, no polygamous society has ever been a true liberal democracy, in anything like the modern sense. As societies move away from hierarchy and toward equal opportunity, they leave polygamy behind. They monogamize as they modernize. That may be a coincidence, but it seems more likely to be a logical outgrowth of the arithmetic of polygamy.

Polygymy . . .is a zero-sum game that skews the marriage market so that some men marry at the expense of others.

The Surplus Male

Other things being equal (and, to a good first approximation, they are), when one man marries two women, some other man marries no woman. When one man marries three women, two other men don't marry. When one man marries four women, three other men don't marry. Monogamy gives everyone a shot at marriage. Polygyny, by contrast, is a zero-sum game that skews the marriage market so that some men marry at the expense of others.

For the individuals affected, losing the opportunity to marry is a grave, even devastating, deprivation. (Just ask a gay American.) But the effects are still worse at the social level. Sexual imbalance in the marriage market has no good social consequences and many grim ones.

Two political scientists, Valerie M. Hudson and Andrea M. den Boer, ponder those consequences in their 2004 book *Bare Branches: Security Implications of Asia's Surplus Male Population*. Summarizing their findings in a *Washington Post* article, they write: "Scarcity of women leads to a situation in which men with advantages—money, skills, education—will marry, but men without such advantages—poor, unskilled, illiterate—will not. A permanent subclass of bare branches [unmarriageable men] from the lowest socioeconomic classes is created. In China and India, for example, by the year 2020 bare branches will make up 12 to 15 percent of the young adult male population."

The problem in China and India is sex-selective abortion (and sometimes infanticide), not polygamy; where the marriage market is concerned, however, the two are functional equivalents. In their book, Hudson and den Boer note that "bare branches are more likely than other males to turn to vice and violence." To get ahead, they "may turn to appropriation of resources, using force if necessary." Such men are ripe for recruitment by gangs, and in groups they "exhibit even more exaggerated risky and violent behavior." The result is "a significant increase in societal, and possibly intersocietal, violence."

The Male Surplus and Crime

Crime rates, according to the authors, tend to be higher in polygynous societies. Worse, "high-sex-ratio societies are governable only by authoritarian regimes capable of suppressing violence at home and exporting it abroad through colonization or war." In medieval Portugal, "the regime would send bare branches on foreign adventures of conquest and colonization." (An equivalent today may be jihad.) In nineteenth-century China, where as many as 25 percent of men were unable to marry, "these young men became natural recruits for bandit gangs and local militia," which nearly toppled the government. In what is now Taiwan, unattached males fomented regular revolts and became "entrepreneurs of violence."

Hudson and den Boer suggest that societies become inherently unstable when sex ratios reach something like 120 males to 100 females: in other words, when one-sixth of men are surplus goods on the marriage market. The United States as a whole would reach that ratio if, for example, 5 percent of men took two wives, 3 percent took three wives, and 2 percent took four wives—numbers that are quite imaginable, if polygamy were legal for a while. In particular communities—inner cities, for example—polygamy could take a toll much more quickly. Even a handful of "Solomons" (high-status men taking multiple wives) could create brigades of new recruits for street gangs and drug lords, the last thing those communities need.

Such problems are not merely theoretical. In northern Arizona, a polygamous Mormon sect has managed its surplus males by dumping them on the street—literally. The sect, reports *The Arizona Republic*, "has orphaned more than 400 teenagers . . . in order to leave young women for marriage to the older men." The paper goes on to say that the boys "are dropped off in neighboring towns, facing hunger, homelessness, and homesickness, and most cripplingly, a belief in a future of suffering and darkness."

True, in modern America some polygynous marriages would probably be offset by group marriages or chain marriages involving multiple husbands, but there is no way to know how large such an offset might be. And remember: *Every* unbalanced polygynous marriage, other things being equal, leaves some man bereft of the opportunity to marry, which is no small cost to that man.

Polygamy Is Socially Destabilizing

The social dynamics of zero-sum marriage are ugly. In a polygamous world, boys could no longer grow up taking marriage for granted. Many would instead see marriage as a trophy in a sometimes brutal competition for wives. Losers would understandably burn with resentment, and most young men, even those who eventually won, would *fear* losing. Although much has been said about polygamy's inegalitarian implications for women who share a husband, the greater victims of inequality would be men who never become husbands.

By this point it should be obvious that polygamy is, structurally and socially, the opposite of same-sex marriage, not its equivalent. Same-sex marriage stabilizes individuals, couples, communities, and society by extending marriage to many who now lack it. Polygamy destabilizes individuals, couples, communities, and society by withdrawing marriage from many who now have it.

As the public focuses on a subject it has not confronted for generations, the hazards of polygamy are likely to sink in. In time, debating polygamy will remind us why our ancestors were right to abolish it. The question is whether the debate will reach its stride soon enough to prevent polygamy from winning a lazy acquiescence that it in no way deserves.

17

Polygamy Is a Distinctive Religious Practice

Gregory L. Smith

Gregory L. Smith is the author of "Polygamy, Prophets, and Prevarication," a lengthy essay on the Mormon practice of plural marriage during the nineteenth century.

It is difficult to travel back in time and understand why Mormons chose to practice polygamy. Today, obedience to God may seem rather old-fashioned, but this was exactly what led Mormons to practice plural marriages: they believed that it was God's will. Plural marriages allowed Mormon families to raise multiple children within the faith of their church, assuring a new generation of believers and a continuation of the Mormon religion. Polygamy also offered Mormons a belief that separated their church from other Christian groups during the nineteenth century. In a sense, plural marriages served as a test for nineteenth-century Mormons: Were they strong enough to obey the will of God by following a practice of which many Americans disapproved? After a time, polygamy was no longer necessary for the well being of the Mormon church, and the practice was discontinued. But the very fact that early members of the church were willing to put their faith on the line is a testament to their courage.

I have long believed that inside some of the hardest doctrines, deep inside them, are some of the greatest truths and the most precious principles. But these are not to be discov-

Gregory L. Smith, "Polygamy, Prophets, and Prevarication," *FAIR*, 2005. Copyright © 2005 by FAIR. Reproduced by permission. Available at www.fairlds.org/Misc/Polygamy_Prophets_and_Prevarication.pdf.

ered casually or irreverently. Obedience actually brings both blessings and additional knowledge . . .

> *Neal. A Maxwell*
> *[official in Church of Jesus Christ of Latter-day Saints]*

When all the history available has been discussed and dissected, we are left with the question: why did the early [Mormon] Saints practice polygamy? The simple answer seems the best: they did it because they believed that God commanded it.

This historian, and even the believer, may consider this answer vaguely unsatisfactory. The follow-up question begs to be asked: why, then, did God command it?

Obedience remains a fundamental doctrine of the gospel of Christ, and plural marriage was an opportunity to show where one's loyalties ultimately lay.

Obedience and Polygamy

Humility demands that we acknowledge that unless God or His servants tell us why something is done, we are only speculating. At the same time, God has always struck me as the ultimate multitasker—He accomplishes many things with a single act. It may well be that multiple outcomes were intended. What follows is a brief speculative mention, in no particular order, of some of the many "accomplishments" of plural marriage.

Obedience is a notion that is out of fashion, especially among the self-proclaimed "intellectual" critics of the Church. Yet, obedience remains a fundamental doctrine of the gospel of Christ, and plural marriage was an opportunity to show where one's loyalties ultimately lay:

They believe in men and women being married only until death doth them part. That is a very cold affair. We do not believe in being married for time only. We believe in making covenants for eternity, and being associated with our wives and children behind the veil. We have received instructions from the Lord in regard to these things, and we are desirous to carry them out.

Simply learning obedience in all things has its merits, despite such a curriculum's unpopularity among the secularists.

The Covenant of Polygamy

God never introduced the Patriarchal order of marriage with a view to please man in his carnal desires, nor to punish females for anything which they had done; but He introduced it for the express purpose of raising up to His name a royal Priesthood, a peculiar people.

Brigham Young

The Book of Mormon's general condemnation of polygamy is frequently mentioned by critics; its exception to this condemnation is less frequently noted: "For if I will, saith the Lord of Hosts, raise up seed unto me, I will command my people; otherwise they shall hearken unto these things." Clearly, one theological function of polygamy could have been to "raise up" groups of people that would be faithful to God. As [Mormon church scripture] Doctrine and Covenants 132 explains:

Abraham received promises concerning his seed, and of the fruit of his loins—from whose loins ye are, namely, my servant Joseph—which were to continue so long as they were in the world; and as touching Abraham and his seed, out of the world they should continue; both in the world and out of the world should they continue as innumerable as the stars; or, if ye were to count the sand upon the seashore ye could not number them. This promise is yours also, because ye are of Abraham, and the promise was made unto Abraham; and by this law is the continuation of the works of my Father, wherein he glorifieth himself. Go ye, therefore, and do the works of Abraham; enter ye into my law and ye shall be saved. But if ye enter not into my law ye cannot receive the promise of my Father, which he made unto Abraham. God commanded Abraham, and Sarah gave Hagar to Abraham to wife. And why did she do it? Because this was the law; and from Hagar sprang many people. This, therefore, was fulfilling, among other things, the promises.

Thus, descendants from a covenant people may have been part of polygamy's purpose. This scripture also confirms our supposition that plural marriage played multiple roles, since righteous posterity is important, "among other things."

Any family willing to make the sacrifices attendant to plural marriage were unreservedly dedicated to the restored gospel.

Some Church members have presumed that polygamy was thus designed to ensure a larger number of descendants than would be possible under monogamy. This need not be the case: polygamy was . . . an effective tool for "winnowing." Any family willing to make the sacrifices attendant to plural marriage were unreservedly dedicated to the restored gospel. Children raised in such an environment can have had no doubt, from an early age, of their parents' convictions. This effect can only have been magnified by the fact that most Church leaders were in polygamous unions.

Plural marriage served, therefore, to train a "peculiar" generation in devotion to their faith, while sparing them the physical persecution of Ohio, Missouri, or Illinois. The Saints were faced with the question of where their ultimate devotion lay: to Church or country? To God or man? To revelation or convention? Plural marriage cast that choice in stark terms which could not be avoided, and the early members did not shrink from the choice.

The Sociology of Polygamy

[T]he institution of polygamy was the best thing that ever happened to Mormonism, and polygamy's suppression at the hands of the federal government was the next best. . .

Douglas H. Parker

The Church's practice of polygamy became public knowledge in 1852. Organized only 22 years prior, the Church was a young, little understood, and often reviled faith. It drew converts from New England, Canada, Scandinavia, England, Scotland, Wales, and elsewhere. Sometimes not even sharing a language, it was necessary that this mix of new members be molded into a solid, enduring social group.

This was accomplished via two means: geographic isolation in the Salt Lake basin and marital practices that were odious to most Americans.

Geographical isolation had become necessary for the Saints' safety. Yet, as [author] Terryl Givens has demonstrated at length, there was little aside from their theology which separated the Saints from general American society. Polygamy served as the perfect dividing line between "Gentile" and "Zion" America. The Saints remained relatively isolated until the coming of the railroad to Utah; by this time their status as a distinct religious and social "culture" was assured, given that they had spent most of the past half century in conflict with the U.S. government over polygamy. Furthermore, intensification of the "polygamy war" in the late 1800s ensured that the arrival of the railroad did not lead to sudden assimilation.

We do not have to look far to discover the fate of a religion without the twin isolators of plural marriage and geography: the Reorganized Church of Jesus Christ of Latter-day Saints [RLDS]. This break-off from the Utah "Brighamites" initially shared most of the other distinctive LDS doctrines, including a belief in Joseph Smith's prophetic call, the divine origin of the Book of Mormon, and a need for a restoration. Yet, today the RLDS Church—now "Communities of Christ"—

has little to distinguish it theologically from mainline Protestantism. Theologically, they were steadily absorbed into the American "mainstream," while the Utah Mormons have retained their separate theological identity, despite joining the American *cultural* mainstream.

However, it was equally important that plural marriage eventually cease, for similar sociological reasons. Even if Utah had successfully given legal protection to plural marriage, it would have stunted Church expansion and growth into other areas. Canada is a good example of a country which moved swiftly to implement antipolygamy statutes upon the arrival of Mormon colonists. Canadian law even went so far as to name Church members as specific legislative targets. Polygamy had served its sociologic purpose by the turn of the century, and world-wide expansion became more feasible with its discontinuation.

No impartial study of the Saints' sacrifices during the polygamy period can fail to impress us with their devotion.

Polygamy and the Abrahamic Test

We complain sometimes about our trials: we need not do that. These are things that are necessary for our perfection. We think sometimes that we are not rightly treated, and I think we think correctly about some of these things. We think there are plots set on foot to entrap us; and I think we think so very correctly.

John Taylor

No impartial study of the Saints' sacrifices during the polygamy period can fail to impress us with their devotion. Doctrine and Covenants 132 acknowledged at the outset that what was being asked was a staggering sacrifice: "Abraham was commanded to offer his son Isaac; nevertheless, it was written:

Thou shalt not kill. Abraham, however, did not refuse, and it was accounted unto him for righteousness."

The command to sacrifice Isaac is one of the most provocative passages of all scripture. It likely holds little interest to the modern humanist except as a case study in religious excess. Even modern Christians—in or out of the Church—perhaps pass over it too glibly. We seem almost over-anxious to reassure ourselves that God didn't *really* intend for Isaac to be sacrificed, and then hasten to draw parallels with God's sacrifice of His Son.

In our haste, however, we miss the fact that God's sacrifice of Christ had a coherent theological rationale, while Abraham received no such justification. Knowing the end of the story, we derive comfort from the ram in the thicket, while Abraham had no such comfort. Latter-day Saints who believe that Jehovah rescued Abraham from being a sacrificial victim himself should also appreciate that the sacrifice of Isaac demanded that Abraham renounce what was doubtless a cherished tenet of his faith: "no human sacrifice."

At its core, polygamy asked the Saints to put their "money where their mouths were."

As the philosopher Søren Kierkegaard described it, in his stimulating study of this scripture, "all was lost, more terrible than if it had never been!. . . Through a miracle [God] had made the preposterous come true [by Isaac's birth to the aged Sarah], now he would see it again brought to nothing."

Kierkegaard puts his finger squarely on the key issue:

What is [generally] left out of the Abraham story is the anguish; for while I am under no obligation to money [which I am asked to sacrifice], to a son the father has the highest and most sacred obligations . . . Abraham's relation to Isaac, ethically speaking, is quite simply this, that the father should love the son more than himself . . . a temptation is [usually] something that keeps a person from carrying out a duty, but here the temptation is the ethical itself which would keep him from doing God's will.

Polygamy and God's Will

Nor should we attribute this doctrine to a mere Old Testament caprice, as Jesus made clear. The Saints were asked to put everything on the altar. For them, "faith was a task for a whole lifetime, not a skill thought to be acquired in either days or weeks." They were not asked simply to part with their sins and foibles, to which anyone might bid a none-too-fond farewell. Beside these offerings they were to then lay their good name, their reputation for moral rectitude and honesty, their civil rights, and their place in American society. Not only must they abandon the false doctrines of the sectarians, but they must appear to renounce cherished principles of monogamy which were viewed as the well-spring of civilization. And then they were later required to discontinue the practice for which they had given so much. The insight of Helen Mar Whitney [twenty-sixth woman to marry Joseph Smith, founder of the Mormon church] is appropriate to this point:

> Those who have not the knowledge and assurance that the course which they are pursuing is according to the will of God, cannot endure all these afflictions and persecutions, taking joyfully the spoiling of their goods and even if necessary to suffer death, by the hands of their foes. They will grow weary and faint and fall by the way unless they have unshaken confidence and a perfect knowledge for themselves. They cannot make a sacrifice of their character and reputation; and give up their houses, their lands, brothers, sisters, wives and children; counting all things as dross, when compared with the eternal life and exaltation, which our Savior has promised to the obedient; and this knowledge is not obtained without a struggle nor the glory without a sacrifice of all earthly things. In the last days (we read) the Lord is to gather together his Saints who have made

covenant with Him by sacrifice and each one must know that their sacrifice is accepted as did righteous, Abel and Abraham the father of the faithful. Every Latter-day Saint knows this to be true, and that according to our faith so are our blessings and privileges.

At its core, polygamy asked the Saints to put their "money where their mouths were." Was Joseph really a prophet, or not? Did prophetic authority persist? Could God truly speak by divine, unmistakable revelation to each individual? Was God's voice truly sovereign over all institutions, and in all circumstances? Were they confident that they could discern that voice, even—or especially—when something contrary to their expectations was demanded?

The Saints' actions answered in the affirmative. I do not envy the ethical extremity in which they found themselves. I am humbly reverent, however, before their moral maturity. Their example makes me uneasy—not because I think I will be asked to resume plural marriage, or because I am troubled by their choices. But, all believers must ultimately mimic Abraham on Mount Moriah. What good must I ultimately leave on the altar, while rejoicing in the only Good?

Organizations to Contact

American Civil Liberties Union (ACLU)
125 Broad St., 18th Floor, New York, NY   10004
(212) 549-2500 • Fax: (212) 549-2646
E-mail: aclu@aclu.org
Web site: www.aclu.org

The ACLU is a national organization that defends Americans' civil rights as guaranteed in the U.S. Constitution. It advocates for freedom of all forms of speech, including pornography, flag burning, and political protest. The ACLU offers numerous reports, fact sheets, and policy statements on free-speech issues, which are available on its Web site. Some of these publications include "Free Speech Under Fire," "Freedom of Expression," and, for students, "Ask Sybil Liberty About Your Right to Free Expression."

Americans United for the Separation of Church and State (AU)
518 C Street NE, Washington, DC   20002
(202) 466-3234 • Fax: (202) 466-2587
Web site: www.au.org

Americans United (AU) defends separation of church and state in the courts, educates legislators, works with the media to inform Americans about religious freedom issues, and organizes local chapters all over the country. The AU's membership is nonsectarian and nonpartisan, and includes Christians, Jews, Buddhists, and people with no religious affiliation; Democrats, Republicans, and independents.

Canadian Association for Free Expression (CAFE)

P.O. Box 332 Station B, Etobicoke
Ontario M9W 5L3, Canada
(905) 897-7221 • Fax: (905) 277-3914
E-mail: cafe@canadafirst.net
Web site: www.canadianfreespeech.com

CAFE, one of Canada's leading civil liberties groups, works to strengthen freedom of speech and freedom of expression provisions in the Canadian Charter of Rights and Freedoms. It lobbies politicians and researches threats to freedom of speech. Publications include specialized reports, leaflets, and *The Free Speech Monitor*, published ten times per year.

Concerned Women for America

1015 Fifteenth St. NW, Suite 1100, Washington, DC   20005
(202) 488-7000 • Fax: (202) 488-0806
E-mail: mail@csfa.org
Web site: www.cwfa.org

CWA works to strengthen marriage and the traditional family according to Judeo-Christian moral standards. It opposes abortion, pornography, homosexuality, and the legalization or decriminalization of prostitution. The organization publishes numerous brochures and policy papers as well as *Family Voice*, a monthly news magazine. Selected articles opposing the legalization or decriminalization of prostitution such as "Trafficking of Women and Children" are available at the organization's Web site.

Duncan Black Macdonald Center for Christian-Muslim Relations

Macdonald Center, Hartford Seminary, Hartford, CT   06105
(860) 509-9534 • Fax: (860) 509-9539
Web site: http://macdonald.hartsem.edu/

The Macdonald Center challenges academics, students, the media, and the general public to develop an accurate awareness and appreciation of Islamic culture. All Macdonald Center faculty and personnel are committed to the importance of better understanding between and among faiths, and to supporting efforts toward building relationships based on tolerance and trust. The Macdonald Center also publishes the quarterly journal, *Muslim World.*

Family Research Council (FRC)
801 G Street NW, Washington, DC   20001
(202) 393-2100 • Fax: (202) 393-2134
Web site: www.frc.org

FRC is a faith-based organization that seeks to promote marriage and family. The FRC attempts to shape public debate and formulates policy that values human life and upholds the institutions of marriage and family. The FRC publishes a variety of books, policy papers, fact sheets, and other materials, including *The Natural Family: A Manifesto* by Allan C. Carlson and Paul T. Mero.

First Amendment Center at Vanderbilt University
1207 18th Ave. S., Nashville, TN   37212
(615) 727-1600 • Fax: (615) 727-1319
E-mail: info@fac.org
Web site: www.firstamendmentcenter.org/

The First Amendment Center works to preserve and protect First Amendment freedoms through information and education. The center serves as a forum for the study and exploration of free-expression issues, including freedom of speech, of the press, and of religion, and the rights to assemble and to petition the government.

Freedom Forum
555 Pennsylvania Ave., NW, Washington, DC   20001
(202) 292-6100 • Fax: (202) 292-6265
E-mail: news@freedomforum.org
Web site: www.freedomforum.org

The Freedom Forum was founded in 1991 to defend a free press and free speech. It operates the Newseum (a museum of news and the news media) and the First Amendment Center, which works to educate the public about free speech and other First Amendment issues. Its publications include, "A Parent's Guide to Religion in the Public Schools."

Human Rights Watch
350 Fifth Ave., 34th Floor, New York, NY   10118-3299
(212) 290-4700 • Fax: (212) 736-1300
E-mail: hrwnyc@hrw.org
Web site: www.hrw.org

Founded in 1978, this nongovernmental organization conducts systematic investigations of human rights abuses in countries around the world, including sex trafficking. It publishes many books and reports on specific countries such as "Mexico's National Human Rights Commission," and covers issues as well as publishing annual reports, recent selections of which are available on its Web site.

Ontario Consultants for Religious Tolerance
P.O. Box 128, Watertown, NY   13601-0128
Web site: www.religioustolerance.org/flds.htm

The Ontario Consultants for Religious Tolerance (OCRT) is a multifaith group. The OCRT believes that systems of truth in the field of morals, ethics, and religion are not absolute and vary by culture, by religion, and over time. The OCRT also believes in the separation of church and state and the freedoms of speech, association, and expression.

Tapestry Against Polygamy
P.O. Box 575782, Murray, UT   84157
801-259-5200
Web site: www.polygamy.org/releases.shtml

The name "Tapestry of Polygamy" was introduced at the organization's first meeting, underlining the fact that each woman who has lived a polygamous lifestyle has woven a unique story. While each Tapestry Against Polygamy member arrives from an individual background, the organization shares an overwhelming desire to help liberate families adversely affected by polygamy.

TruthBearer.org

P.O. Box 765, Old Orchard Beach, ME 04064
Web site: www.truthbearer.org

An infrastructure devoted to Christian polygamy, TruthBearer-.org is an independent organization that provides support and ministry for various independent Christ-centered individuals, groups, and ministries. Scripture-based and cross-denominational, TruthBearer.org works proactively to bring Christian polygamy to churches, Christian colleges, pastors, leaders, and other Christ-centered organizations and ministries.

U.S. Department of Justice

810 Seventh St. NW, Washington, DC 20531
(202) 514-2000
Web sites: www.usdoj.gov • www.ojp.usdoj.gov/bjs/welcome.html

The Department of Justice protects citizens by maintaining effective law enforcement, crime prevention, crime detection, and prosecution and rehabilitation of offenders. Through its Office of Justice Programs, the department operates the National Institute of Justice, the Office of Juvenile Justice and Delinquency Prevention, and the Bureau of Justice Statistics. Its publications include fact sheets, research packets, bibliographies, and the semiannual journal *Juvenile Justice.*

Women's Commission on Refugee Women and Children

122 East 42nd St., New York, NY 10168-1289
(212) 551-3115 • Fax: (212) 551-3180
E-mail: info@womenscommission.org
Web site: www.womenscommission.org

The commission offers solutions and provides technical assistance to ensure that refugee women, children, and adolescents are protected and have access to education, health services, and livelihood opportunities. It makes recommendations to U.S. and United Nations policy makers and nongovernmental organizations on ways to improve assistance to refugee women and children. Experts conduct field research and technical training in refugee camps and detention centers. On its Web site the commission publishes issues of its semiannual newsletter, *Women's Commission News*, reports, and articles, including "The Struggle Between Migration Control and Victim Protection: The U.K. Approach to Human Trafficking."

Bibliography

Books

Benjamin G. Bistline — *Colorado City Polygamists: An Inside Look for the Outsider.* Scottsdale, AZ: Agreka Books, 2004.

Brian C. Hales — *Modern Polygamy and Mormon Fundamentalism: The Generations After the Manifesto.* Salt Lake City, UT: Greg Kofford Books, 2007.

B. Carmon Hardy, Editor — *Doing The Works of Abraham: Mormon Polygamy: Its Origin, Practice, and Demise* (Kingdom in the West: the Mormons and the American Frontier, Volume 9). Norman, OK: Arthur H. Clark Company, 2007.

Carolyn Jessop and Laura Palmer — *Escape.* New York: Broadway, 2007.

Philip L. Kilbride — *Plural Marriage for Our Times: A Reinvented Option?* Westport, CT: Bergin & Garvey, 1994.

John R. Llewellyn — *Murder of a Prophet: The Dark Side of Utah Polygamy.* Scottsdale, AZ: Agreka Books, 2000.

John R. Llewellyn — *Polygamy's Rape of Rachael Strong.* Scottsdale, AZ: Agreka Books, 2006.

John R. Llewellyn — *A Teenager's Tear: When Parents Convert to Polygamy.* Scottsdale AZ: Agreka Books, 2001.

David G. Maillu   *Our Kind of Polygamy*. Nairobi, Kenya: East African Education Publication, 2000.

Andrea Moore-Emmett   *God's Brothel: The Extortion of Sex for Salvation in Contemporary Mormon and Christian Fundamentalist Polygamy and the Stories of 18*. San Francisco, CA: Pince-Nez Press, 2004.

Susan Ray Schmidt   *His Favorite Wife: Trapped in Polygamy*. Twin Falls, ID: Kassidy Lane Publishing, 2006.

Dorothy Allred Solomon   *Daughter of the Saints: Growing Up In Polygamy*. New York: W.W. Norton & Company, 2004.

Dorothy Allred Solomon   *Predators, Prey, and Other Kinfolk: Growing Up in Polygamy*. New York: W.W. Norton & Company, 2003.

Irene Spencer   *Shattered Dreams: My Life as a Polygamist's Wife*. New York: Center Street, 2007.

Richard S. Van Wagoner   *Mormon Polygamy: A History*. Salt Lake City, UT: Signature Books, 1992.

Periodicals

"Activists Lobby for Stricter Laws Against Polygamy in Arizona," *Arizona Capitol Times*, February 1, 2008.

"The Advocate Poll," *Advocate*, July 4, 2006.

Rebecca Ascher Walsh · "Love Is in the Air: The Implications of HBO's Nighttime Drama About Polygamy," ADWEEK, July 9, 2007.

"Back in Fashion; Polygamy," *Economist* (US), December 2, 2006.

Andrew Billen · "As American as Apple Pie: A Subtle Satire on Polygamy Reveals the Secret Oddness of Every Family," *New Statesman* (1996), June 26, 2006.

Laura Blue · "The Merry Wives: A Longtime Haven of Polygamy Is Feeling the Heat from Police," *Time Canada*, October 10, 2005.

Kathy and Jan Brown · "I Grew Up in a Polygamist Family," *Today's Christian Woman*, Nov.-Dec. 2006.

Kim Burgess · "Strange Bedfellows: Polygamy and Same-Sex Marriage Get Uncomfortably Close," *Curve*, Jan.-Feb. 2007.

Michelle Cottle · "Two-Timing: Life Lessons from 'Big Love,'" *New Republic*, May 22, 2006.

Anthony Daniels · "Polygamy Ascendant? Rumbles in Our Marriage Debate," *National Review*, September 25, 2006.

Brianne
Goodspeed

"Stewardship and Recreation: Is This a Marriage Made in Utah?," *E*, Jan.-Feb. 2007.

Greg Hernandez

"Big Gay Love," *Advocate*, June 6, 2006.

Kirk Johnson

"Utah: The Perfect Genetics Lab," *New York Times Upfront*, February 14, 2005.

"Live Fast, Love Hard, Die Young; Evolution," *Economist* (US), October 20, 2007.

Ken MacQueen

"Polygamy: Legal in Canada," *Maclean's*, June 25, 2007.

"Mormon Polygamy: An Interview with the Author of God's Brothel," *off our backs*, March 2006.

Gina Passarella

"Right to Teach Polygamy to Child Protected (Shepp v. Shepp)," *Legal Intelligencer*, September 29, 2006.

Elise Soukup

"Polygamists, Unite!" *Newsweek*, March 20, 2006.

Joe Strupp

"Readers Show 'Big Love' for Utah Polygamy Beat," *Editor & Publisher*, August 16, 2007.

Joe Treasure

"Polygamy: Wives and Republicans," *New Statesman* (1996), September 24, 2007.

Index